GREAT FISHING IN LAKE ERIE & TRIBUTARIES

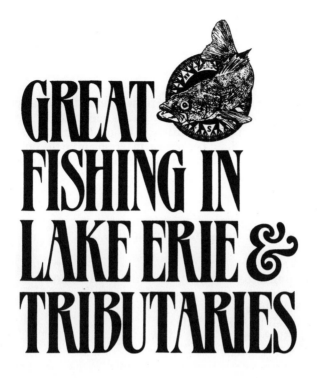

GREAT FISHING IN LAKE ERIE & TRIBUTARIES

Will Elliott

Northeast Sportsman's Press
Tarrytown, New York

Stackpole Books
Harrisburg, Pennsylvania

Library of Congress Cataloging-In-Publication Data

Elliott, Will.
    Great fishing in Lake Erie & Tributaries / Will Elliott.
    p. cm.
    ISBN 0-8117-4036-6
    1. Fishing—Erie, Lake. I. Title
    SH464.E75E43 1991
    799. 1'1'097712—dc20   90-26859
                                                                        CIP

All photographs by Will Elliott except as noted

Published by Stackpole Books and
Northeast Sportsman's Press

Distributed by Stackpole Books
Cameron & Kelker Sts.
Harrisburg, PA 17105

Printed in the United States of America

10-9-8-7-6-5-4-3-2-1

ABOUT THE AUTHOR

Born too late for Lake Erie's blue pike heyday, Will Elliott spent many evenings awaiting the chance to get out on the big lake's open waters off the Town of Evans shoreline, where the propane lanterns of fishermen blinked temptingly on the horizon. The happy (though polluted) days of the late 1950's on Lake Erie meant, for most, finding and catching yellow perch and smallmouth bass along any and all rock drop-offs.

Through high school and college, he set aside as many days as possible for fishing the ever changing Erie. English and Education majors at The University at Buffalo and Canisius College further enhanced an interest in both teaching and writing about the sport of fishing.

Teaching English at Depew High School for more than 25 years and contributing to New York Sea Grant's Speakers Bureau offered many opportunities to develop further contacts for Lake Erie fisheries.

A twelve-year stint as fishing class instructor only heightened a desire to interest more adults and youngsters in the sport of fishing. While developing materials for these fishing classes, he expanded many topics to serve as magazine articles.

A busy period of freelance article writing led to his selection as writer of the weekly "Fishing Line" column in the Buffalo News (daily circulation 340,000). The column has appeared for five years and may be seen in every Friday issue.

This book is yet another "end product" of the author's extensive interest in fishing in general and Lake Erie in particular.

ACKNOWLEDGEMENTS

First acknowledgement must go to Lake Erie itself for its survival through man's long era of misuse and neglect. Inspiration for this book came mainly from the realization that, despite all the abuse and indifference, Lake Erie continued to support tons of catchable fish even when most considered it a "dead" lake.

To Jean, my wife and eternal editor, who saw to it that every page made some sense and told the truth with a minimum of spelling errors, I extend a big thank you. Now she wants to get out for a few perch — she's earned it.

Many of the following people have spent their lives studying and working on Lake Erie. Although no list of credits can include all people worthy of note, I especially want to thank:

Don Einhouse, Floyd Cornelius, Steve Mooradian, Bill Shepherd, David O. Kelch, Fred L. Snyder, Carl T. Baker, Randy Eshenroder, Sheryl Hood, Bob Haas, Dan Thomas, Sam Concilla, Doug Case, Tom Scott, Harry Keppner, Capt. Ken Kuczka, Capt. Bob Jaycox (and his wife Virginia and son Jr.), and Capt. Kevin Caffery.

And finally, here is a partial list of on-the-water friends who have shared Lake Erie information with zeal and accuracy:

James Archie, Frank "Dusty" Amborski, John Abbatoy, Tony Anderson, Dave Barus, Dave Bianchi, Don Bruning, Dick Bennett, Frank Becker, Andy Bogulski, Paul Cybart, Capt. Jim Catalano, Warren Caldwell, Al Cretacci, Roger Drollinger, Fran Dollard, Capt. Dan Dietzen, Ted Depczynski, Capt. Ron Drozdowski, Don David, Joe Fisher, Joe Forma, Capt. Pat Fox, Bill Frey, Dennis Gowan, Jim Greco, Jack Gerome, Jim Grevin, Gary Geartz, Bill Hilts Sr. and Bill Hilts Jr., Bob Hauser, Jim Hanley, Doug Hurtubise, Rusty Haines, Hank Kurowski, Capt. Jerry Heffernan, Gene Izzie, Capt. Bonnie Krieger, Jim Kassman, Russ Johnson, Rick Kinecki, Mark Kubicki, Ed Kulczynski, Fred Kokot, Don Kraft, Lou Krygier, Jim and Sue Lawniczak, Jim Lindstrom, Mike Levy, Capt. Rich Lazarczyk, Capt. Pete Latka, Dennis Landahl, Ken and Ginger Macijewski, Jerry Hans, Paul Mekeown, Paul Megyes, Bob Malinowski, Rick Miller, Phil Mazur, Ted and

Doraine Malota, Capt. Dave Marino, Bob Naab, Gary and John Pinzel, Dave Peterson, John Powell, Mike Pratko, Joe Peters, Carl Rozek, Charles Rechlin, Don Reukauf, Bud Riser, Jim Reynolds, Art Roland, Capt. Bob Rustowicz, Lou Stefan, Ed Soda, Dick Smith, John Spagnoli, Herb Schultz, Capt. Todd Selbert, Capt. Dick Sprague, Perry Sprague, Dick and Rick Schleyer, Jerry Sloma, Joe Smith, Jim Ehrig, Tom Slomka, Pat and Bill VanCamp, Tom Vandeveld, Mike Voiland, Capts. Lou and Walter Will, Mike Wilkinson, Rod Watson, Walter Wrzesinski, Jerry Zywiczynski, and Capt. Dennis Zukowski.

To these and hundreds of other Lake Erie fishermen who struggled to "bring Erie back," thank you. Your spirit has helped make this book a joy to write.

TABLE OF CONTENTS

TEXT NOTES

A number of words and phrases used in this book are somewhat technical or are localisms which have gained almost universal usage among anglers along the Lake Erie shoreline. These definitions, some annotated, may help you to better understand the fish and fishing described in this book.

Bass - Generally a reference to smallmouth bass. While largemouth bass can be found in selected bays and harbors, smallmouth bass dominate the Lake Erie fishery.

Blue Pike - Once abundant in Lake Erie, particularly over deeper waters in the Eastern Basin of Lake Erie, this subspecies of the walleye was declared extinct by the Province of Ontario in 1986 and entered as extinct in the Federal Register by the U.S. Fish and Wildlife Service on September 2, 1983.

Breakline - The line formed between a gradual and a sudden drop-off. Look for the line that separates widely spaced parallel lines and much more narrowly spaced lines on a topographical map. Look for a continuous, sharp drop-off — generally parallel to shore in shallower areas — when reading a sonar (flasher or graph) or when afloat in search of fish-holding structure.

Breakwater - Any man-made structure (parallel to or perpendicular with shore) designed to protect the shoreline and provide safe-harbor areas for navigation.

Catch-and-Release Fishing - A conservation-minded approach to fishing in which anglers kill either no fish or a limited number of fish. Fish — especially the larger breeders — are released after a quick picture-taking session. Catch-and-Release has been slow to develop in Lake Erie waters, because of the remarkable abundance of "eating size" fish of many species in all areas of the lake.

Central Basin - The U.S. waters of Lake Erie along the north central and eastern section of Ohio. Roughly, this basin is bounded by the Huron/Vermilion area at the western end and the Ohio/Pennsylvania state boundary line at the eastern end. Its shorelines support the largest human population, greatest amount of industry and the greatest amount of both access sites and shoreline mileage.

Charter boat - Any boat, piloted by a licensed captain, which is rented for a half day, day or longer to fish for a specific fish with particular techniques. Charters usually take parties of up to six persons.

Culling - Selecting the more desirable (usually larger) fish and releasing the smaller fish. In tournament fishing, culling is when smaller fish are removed and released from a live well in order to comply with tournament limits. In recreational fishing, culling is a means of practicing catch-and-release fishing for all species of fish.

DEC - Abbreviation for New York State's Department of Environmental Conservation.

DNR - Abbreviation for Department of Natural Resources. The fisheries management and enforcement organization for the states of Ohio and Michigan.

Eastern Basin - That portion of Lake Erie bounded by the New York shoreline (Buffalo to Barcelona), but extending west to include the City of Erie and much of the northwestern section of Pennsylvania.

Fancast - A deliberate pattern of casting in a continuing circle to cover as much water as possible and to determine the direction(s) in which fish strike the cast lure. This is a favored technique when fishing on board a head boat in the western and central basins of Lake Erie.

Forage - (both a noun and a verb) n. Any food source for aquatic life. With the extremes of depth and water temperature found in Lake Erie, both warm- and cold-water forage offer a food source for both warm- and cold-water species of gamefish in the eastern basin. v. Means by which gamefish seek food. Lake Erie is noted for both bottom-relating fish, and suspended fish foraging at varying depths.

Flipping - (aka "flippin'") More a means of swinging than casting a lure in an underhand fashion such that the lure can be placed in close, specific locations. Special rods and reels have been designed for flipping, but most medium and medium-heavy casting or spinning rods will serve well. This technique allows for casting around docks, piers, and other shoreline structures which often hold fish but do not allow for overhead casting.

Head boat - Fishing vessels which hire out to individuals or, less commonly, groups. Anglers may board on a walk-on basis (without reservations) until the maximum allowable number of passengers are aboard. Hence, the name "head" boat. Head boats usually offer non-boat owners the least expensive way to get out for a day of fishing. Also known as party boat.

LCD - (Liquid Crystal Display) General term for screen-type depth finders which simulate scrolling readouts of depth and water conditions as shown on conventional paper graphs.

Lure tuning - Any means of altering a lure so that it moves more effectively through the water and attracts more fish. Despite some manufacturer claims, virtually every artificial bait (lure, plug, etc.) can be improved by tuning: changing leader-to-weight leader lengths, adjusting angle of front eye, turning and/or trimming hooks, etc.

Pattern - Any combination of factors that leads to the successful taking of fish. Weather conditions, bottom structure, water temperature, specialized tackle items and techniques are all common components of any pattern. Patterns can help to replicate past successes, but they should always be considered guidelines rather than absolute formulas.

pH - A measure of the acidity or alkalinity of water. A "neutral" reading (pH 7) is considered an ideal level for many fish. Runoff, rainfall, bottom sedimentation and many other conditions affect the pH factor of water.

Perch - Common term for the yellow perch. Lake Erie supports large schools of white perch and white "silver" bass, but the staple species is the yellow perch.

Reef - An underwater structure which rises close to the surface. Such structures in Lake Erie have long been identified as either reefs or shoals with no apparent distinction as to size, configuration, composition, etc. For example, try to determine why all those structures off Davis-Besse between A-Can and F-Can are called a "Reef" in the Western Basin and why Waverly Shoal in the Eastern Basin is called a shoal [see "Shoal"].

Rip rap - Any formation of loosely piled rock structures either man-made or formed by nature. Openings formed between the rocks provide protection for forage species and attract a variety of larger fish which feed on that bait.

Shoal - A place in any body of water where the water is especially shallow. Many of the places called a "reef" would also qualify as a "shoal". It is much more important to find these fish-holding areas in Lake Erie than to worry about any distinction between them.

Stickbait - Originally designed as a slender, floating, minnow-type bait used for casting, the term "stickbait" now generally applies to any cigar-shaped crankbait (shallow-running or deep-diving) which is used in trolling rigs.

Structure - Any marked change in depth anywhere on the bottom of a lake. Included would be breaklines, sunken islands, reefs and shoals. Before the widespread use of sonar equipment, expert Erie anglers would always say "look for the drop-offs." Depth changes as slight as one or two feet will often hold heavy schools of bait and game fish.

Suspended fish - Game fish drawn away from bottom "cover" to depths in open water. Ideal water conditions, available forage or a combination of the two will draw fish — many of which are associated with bottom structures — to hold at suspended depths.

Thermocline - A pronounced layer of water marked by a sudden change of temperature, generally a three-degree or greater change in water temperature within a one-foot change in depth. Thermoclines form (are "set up") in many temperate-zone lakes during the warmer months and separate the generally stable lower waters and the generally unstable waters nearer the surface. Many modern-day sonar units will record suspended plant and animal particles which hold in thermoclines. Fishermen look for it in order to find schools of forage and gamefish, which often are found in or just above the thermocline.

Vertical jigging - Long associated with ice fishing on Lake Erie, this technique is seeing a steady increase each warm-water season. Weighted lures such as body baits or spoons are sent to the bottom and worked up and down in a variety of ways.

Walleye - Popular perch family, pike-shaped fish often called "yellow pike" or even "pike" by local anglers. Tagging studies indicate that walleye exhibit extremes in behavior: some inhabit one finite area, feeding and reproducing within its confinement; others forage widely, at times traveling hundreds of miles in search of food between spawning cycles.

Weed line - Any line formed along the outer edge of a weed mass. Weed lines change radically as the summer season begins. Fish movement around weed lines can be drastically affected by changes in pH and oxygenation of these relatively shallow waters.

Western Basin - The "islands" area of the lake west of Vermilion/Huron. The Western Basin extends west to Maumee Bay and Toledo Harbor, and it includes waters in the state of Michigan between Toledo and the Detroit River.

INTRODUCTION

One big consideration when discussing the new Lake Erie is overcoming the negative image of the old Lake Erie, a lake that was heavily burdened with industrial waste plus the effluent and excesses of the burgeoning human population found along its shoreline. Everyone can recall at least one good joke about Lake Erie or its fish or the cities along its shores. Things have improved dramatically.

Long the dumping ground for solid and liquid wastes from commercial, industrial, municipal and private sources, Lake Erie prevailed through many decades of misuse and neglect. Not only did the lake and its aquatic life remain viable, but it actually supported great numbers of fish even when many considered the lake either "fished out" or polluted to a point beyond saving.

In fact one species, the blue pike, gradually disappeared from its waters. But many of the other food fish (bass, walleye and yellow perch) maintained a solid presence and even began to increase in numbers as pollution levels decreased. The addition of stocked salmonids (principally coho salmon, rainbow and brown trout) adds even more to the bounty that is Lake Erie's fishery today.

"Stories" in this book will be kept to a minimum. However, every sign of an improved Lake Erie fishery makes for yet another good one. One of my favorites was told quite vividly by Toni Orsini in the August, 1990 issue of *The Fishline* — newsletter of the Southtowns Walleye Association of Western New York. Orsini, one of the few regular fishermen who fished Lake Erie exclusively in the early 1970's, gives this account:

I had just lost my last Yellow Sally on a snag at the slag pile behind the steel plant drifting into Smokes Creek. After a few choice words I reeled in my line, started the motor and headed to Strohm's Marina where my Uncle Emil Orsini had rented boats and sold bait and tackle. The Small Boat Harbor was just about the only place you could launch a boat if you were from

xix

South Buffalo. It was back in the summer of '71. When I got home I pulled out the S.O.S. pads, a pail of Tide water and began cleaning off the orange, slimy film that told everyone that you were fishing near Smokes Creek. It would take about four hours to get the boat looking good again. That was excellent because when I lost my last Yellow Sally, in the heat of anger I vowed never to fish Lake Erie again and to sell the boat. I had lots of reasons — the blue pike were gone, eight out of ten fish caught were sheepshead, and after the 4th of July the only walleye you were able to muster up were in the evening. I sold.

But that was 20 years ago. Through those years, though, I did hear of a group of anglers and sportsmen who didn't give up and sell. They formed a club called the Southtowns Walleye Association. [Two major walleye groups were formed in Western New York in the early 1980's: the New York Walleye Association and the Southtowns Walleye Association of W.N.Y., Inc. The combined membership of these two associations now exceeds 5,000. ed.]

As the years went by, the efforts of this group plus those of some sincere local elected officials started to make things change. Water got cleaner and the fish were making a comeback. The gill netting bill was passed and more access to the lake was developed.

In February of this year [1990] my son Tony III, who is 22, purchased a 1983 fiberglass boat with an 85 Johnson motor. The first good day this spring we were back behind the steel plant fishing for walleye. It was a little slow because of the cold but I was really impressed with the changes you could see only from a boat.

After a few trips in the boat my adrenalin started flowing. So my son Tony, my two sons-in-law (Dave and Ed) and I joined the Southtowns Walleye Club and Tournament. The sad part is, the day we signed up we didn't sign up for the other club's contest [New York Walleye Association] because it was already in progress for two days. Later my 14-year-old daughter, Joy, landed a 10-pound-plus walleye on a 6-pound test crappie pole with a spinner and worm. That really got the fever going again, with the club's contest in progress; with Joy's fish at the taxidermist; with the way she looked when we would come back from fishing, with that little smile and that "any luck?" tinkle in her voice. On Tuesday, June 19th, with that praise and that look still etched in our brain, Tony, Dave and I decided to go fishing. When we pulled up at the Sturgeon Point Marina, the attendant informed us the Coast Guard had just pulled a capsized boat from the water. I looked at the boys and asked

"What do you want to do?" Not realizing that waves look bigger in a boat than they do from shore, the boys said "let's go". We launched the boat and headed out. As I looked over my shoulder to watch the three to five foot swells head toward shore I noticed Tony and Dave scramble for the life preservers and put them on (good move). Obviously they had more sense than I. After playing with the motor in the bay near the mouth of the marina I noticed the only other boat, with two fishermen, pull out of the marina and head out to the left. Well then, I said to myself and them, it must be OK, let's troll out behind them. With our lines out heading into the waves in 19 feet of water I felt what I first thought was a snag and, to this day, I'm still not sure if we were trolling or still fishing with the motor in gear. As I started to reel in, the open-faced reel I was using snapped in the center of the spool — I could turn the handle once then turn the spool by hand once. When I realized that it was a fish instead of a snag I shut off the motor and started hauling him in. When we finally netted him on the fourth try (I won't tell who was doing the missing with the net) we had drifted past the lighthouse on the Kellogg estate.

The next morning I was at the Tackle Shack, fish on ice, and a smile from ear to ear when I was told he weighed 10.34....

Orsini's 10.34-pound walleye held first place during most of the tourney only to be nosed out by 9/100's of a pound on the last day. His story is typical of the renewed interest in fishing for walleye and many other species of fish in the steadily improving fishable waters of Lake Erie.

His story also points up many other aspects of fishing that will be discussed in this book: the need to know and respect weather conditions at all times, the value of good equipment, a familiarization with the area to be fished, and mastery of the tackle you're using.

No single group has been exclusively responsible for the restored beauty of this bounteous inland sea. It has taken the collective efforts of many people in politics, governmental fisheries bureaus, water-dependent industries, public utility companies, area residents and Lake Erie fishermen themselves. All these men and women deserve high regard for their labors, often given freely and without compensation.

For a thorough list of readable-yet-technical data on Lake Erie, the reader is encouraged to write and ask for the numbered list of "Technical Reports" published by

Great Lakes Fishery Commission
1451 Green Road
Ann Arbor, MI 48105

or "Technical Publications" from

Ohio State University
1314 Kinnear Road
Columbus, OH 43212

Part One

Getting Set to Go

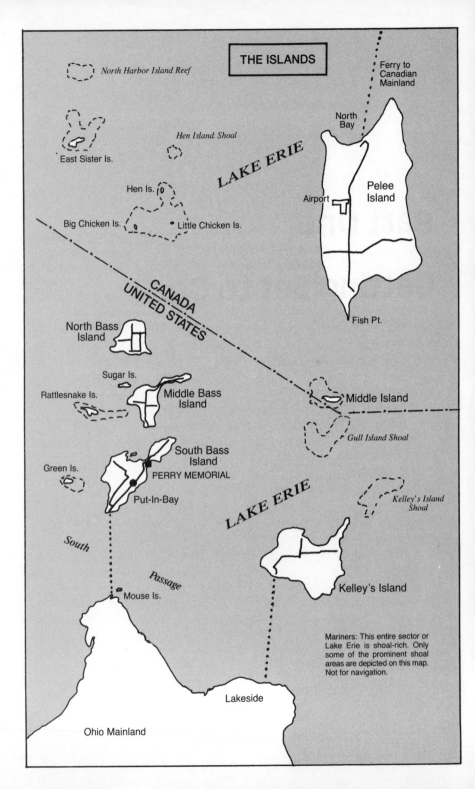

THE ISLANDS

North Harbor Island Reef

East Sister Is.

Hen Island Shoal

LAKE ERIE

Ferry to
Canadian
Mainland

North
Bay

Pelee
Island

Airport

Hen Is.

Big Chicken Is.   Little Chicken Is.

Fish Pt.

CANADA
UNITED STATES

North Bass
Island

Sugar Is.

Rattlesnake Is.   Middle Bass
Island

Middle Island

Gull Island Shoal

Green Is.

South Bass
Island
PERRY MEMORIAL

Put-In-Bay

LAKE ERIE

Kelley's Island
Shoal

South

Passage

Mouse Is.

Kelley's Island

Mariners: This entire sector or
Lake Erie is shoal-rich. Only
some of the prominent shoal
areas are depicted on this map.
Not for navigation.

Lakeside

Ohio Mainland

Chapter 1

General Description and Background

L ong stretches of level sand, sharply rising shale and granite cliffs, fertile farmlands, vast areas of wetlands, long spans of rocky breakwaters: When viewed from the deck of a boat, Lake Erie's shoreline is a scenic mosaic often reminiscent of unspoiled, far-away places.

From Sandusky east to Buffalo, Lake Erie is an unbroken expanse of open water; it is like a sea but it changes with the winds rather than with the tides. During periods of relative calm, the lake waters are vivid green along the shoreline shallows, and a deep blue over the deeper waters of the Central and Western Basins. During periods of high winds and heavy rainfall, long swaths of muddied and stained waters mark the extent of nature's force on Erie's tributary streams and shallower shoreline waters.

Prevailing winds are west to east. At some locations around the lake—or at certain times—the prevailing winds may be from the southwest or northwest. Currents, not always parallel with the prevailing winds, occur even in the shallower sections of the lake. While these currents are not a danger to navigation, they greatly influence the fish and the fishing. Bathymetry charts of the lake show currents moving in a generally clockwise direction in Lake Erie.

Lake Erie has ten sizable islands plus a number of smaller ones. Most of these are located in the southwestern corner of the lake. The largest is Pelee Island, which has its own small airport. Boaters can course around the rocky shoals of the Western Basin passing these islands, many of which are inhabited. Kelley's Island, the second largest in the island group, is surrounded by fish-holding shoals and reefs which extend northwest to north. There are also Middle and South Bass Island; on the latter, Perry's Monument stands proudly on the eastern shore. U.S. Naval Officer Oliver Hazard Perry defeated the British fleet on Lake Erie in 1813.

Erie's fishing is multi-dimensional. Most access sites along the U.S. shoreline are known for two or more of the popular species caught in the lake. It's entirely possible to start fishing for walleye and encounter a heavy school of smallmouth bass, yellow perch, trout, salmon, or other fish not initially targeted.

For the fisherman willing to seek out these opportunities, Lake Erie is a beautiful lake to behold, a great place to take friends and family, and an excellent place to catch good-sized fish in good numbers.

Mentionable Dimensions

Many superlatives can be attributed to Lake Erie, but the most mentionable statistic is a retention rate of only 2.6 years. That means that the entire volume of the lake is replaced (i.e. flushed) in less than three years. In stark contrast to Lake Superior with a retention rate of more than 200 years, Lake Erie clearly has a capacity for rapid ecological change.

Another significant point of comparison with other Great Lakes is that Lake Erie is the shallowest, with a mean depth of only 62 feet. Interpretations vary on this statistic. Being the shallowest, the lake warms fastest and is likely to move more quickly toward eutrophication, the technical term for old age in a lake. Part of the "Dead Sea" image Erie has had stems from the reality that Lake Erie is quite shallow and is thus particularly prone to the ecological aging process. On the other hand, the vast amount of relatively shallow water has the advantage of being able to support many more catchable fish than a lake that has mostly deep, cold water with much of that water well below the thermocline level. In short, Lake Erie's comparatively warm water has the ability to hold a lot of fish.

At 9,930-9,960 square miles, depending on the atlas consulted, Lake Erie ranks second only to Lake Ontario for the least surface area among Great Lakes. With a length of 241 miles and a maximum width of 57 miles, Lake Erie is both small and big. It's less than one third the size of Lake Superior (31,820 square miles), but almost equal in size to the entire state of Vermont.

Lake Erie's maximum depth is 210 feet. It has almost 500 miles of shoreline counting both the U.S. and Canadian sides.

The Detroit, Raisin, Maumee, Huron, Sandusky, Vermilion, Black, Rocky, Cuyahoga, Chagrin, Grand, Ashtabula and Cattaraugus Rivers all flow into Lake Erie on the U.S. side. The Niagara River carries Lake Erie waters over Niagara Falls and into Lake Ontario. All these waterways, plus a few of the larger creeks, are navigable at least part ways up for smaller fishing boats.

The United States shoreline population exceeded 13 million in the 1990 census. Yet a mile from shore, the physical appearance of most of the U.S. shoreline remains natural looking.

Indians to Industries

Erie appears to perennially be a lake in transition. Like the Native Americans who populated its shores, its fortunes have risen and fallen. The League of Five Nations in the Iroquois Confederation (called the Six Nations after 1715) had an ongoing battle with the Hurons, the tribe which occupied much of Lake Erie's north shore. The Erie Tribe, which inhabited the south shore—most of the Ohio and Pennsylvania shoreline—concealed escaping Huron tribesmen from attacks by Five Nations warriors. Because of their compassion, Erie tribesmen were slaughtered to near extinction. Thus, much of Lake Erie's south shoreline appeared uninhabited when European settlers moved in and began developing farmable land sites.

Lake Erie, like the Native American tribe of the same name, once flourished and then nearly disappeared. But while the native culture did sadly disappear, Erie the lake is now making a spectacular comeback.

Native Americans chose the name "Erie" to symbolize the elusive, unpredictable nature of its waters. Erie is the Native American name for "cat". Man domesticated the dog, but a cat often just remains a companionable but untrainable creature, present but never quite tame or explainable.

Early explorers, merchants and settlers used Erie as an avenue to get from place to place. Explorers and traders prided themselves on the speed at which they could cross the midsection of the Great Lakes to claim territories or return with goods. The aim was to do it faster than other explorer-travelers. Robert de La Salle found a quick way to get around the Niagara Falls gorge and up onto Lake Erie waters— a kind of super highway cut through the woods—in order to move west, set up a base with the Illinois tribe and find his way down the Mississippi. Lake Erie served as a wide channel in the passage west.

Settlers-turned-industrialists found Lake Erie an effective vehicle for commerce. With the advent of motor-driven ships, Erie could deliver everything from coal to flour (later, automobiles) in bulk weight much cheaper than could be done over the road. A series of massive concrete silo-like grain elevators still mark the skyline of South Buffalo, where lake freighters once lined up to deliver grain for milling (which continues in Buffalo). Ashtabula, Cleveland and Lorain, Ohio continue to be lake-dependent for the delivery of coal and steel-making products. Big barges, lake freighters and well-equipped fishing boats now share the same waterways.

Once settled, Lake Erie—the shallowest of the five Great Lakes— was always the first to be affected by severe weather and ecological changes. From the indiscriminate discharge of pollutants to the introduction of undesirable aquatic species, Lake Erie has usually led in exhibiting the first signs of ongoing changes, all too frequently changes for the worse.

Public Image
When things go bad, few see any possibility for good. Industrial growth and commercial success and the resultant industrial complexes along the shore gave Lake Erie the image of a factory with no fields, a wasted waterway given over to coal, steel and commerce.

In recent times, Lake Erie was referred to as an inland "Dead Sea."

Buffalo and the Western New York area was once described by a western sports writer as "the armpit of the East." In the early 70's, not many residents were heard pridefully speaking about life along the shores of Lake Erie. Many still recall the comic lines delivered by comedienne Peggy Cass about the Cayahoga River catching fire. President Lyndon Johnson and the First Lady were photographed grimacing at a bucket of putrid water taken from the Buffalo River. That picture was sent out on the national news wires and became the late-60's image of what one might expect when coming upon Lake Erie waters.

Transitional weather patterns, careless indifference about water quality in the first half of the Twentieth Century and the repeated introduction of unwanted aquatic species all had combined to project a most appalling picture of Lake Erie for much of the second half of the twentieth century.

Besides pollution, overfishing also took its toll. In fact, in the opinion of many, excessive commercial and sport harvests between about 1930 and 1960 had a major negative impact. By the late 1950's Lake Erie could not support more than a dozen commercial fish tugs. With the demise of the blue pike and a reduction in the walleye population by 1960, commercial fishermen had to rely mainly on the unpredictable numbers of yellow perch that might be taken in a season's harvest.

Each summer, during the 1960's, fewer commercial fishermen worked the lake on a full-time basis. Many part-time netters quit operations completely. Lake Erie indeed appeared to be a fresh water Dead Sea. The image seemed to hold true.

But Lake Erie's image has begun to rapidly improve in the past two decades. Since the first Earth Day and the countrywide efforts to clean up our nation's air and waters in the early 1970's, Lake Erie has become one of the brightest lights emerging from the darkness of mankind's neglect of and indifference toward fishable waters.

Fingers were pointed at major industries, commercial fishermen, fisheries management agencies, developers, various public works agencies and population increases in general. But in fact, Lake Erie was damaged by all of us collectively using its waters as we wished or needed. Today, Lake Erie is being improved by those same people (all of us) who have become increasingly aware of the vast but vulnerable nature of this great lake.

Lake Erie's comeback is still in its early stages. Every summer, lakefront and near-lakefront land values increase proportionately more than nearby inland properties. Sporting groups, municipalities and private marina operators continually search for means to increase and utilize access for all manner of waterfront activities, principally those relating to boating and fishing. Fishing-related equipment sales and tourism services steadily increase with each discovery of a new facet of Lake Erie's fishing bounty.

Historically, smallmouth bass fishing around any shallow-water structures in late spring and early summer has been Lake Erie's best kept secret. While most other species either declined or disappeared during Erie's "dead" years, the bass were there every season to excite both the newest and the most experienced of anglers. Small boats and basic hand-held tackle items were all that was needed to get bass. Nearshore sites repeatedly offered excellent sport to anyone willing to get out and give the bass a try.

Then came the deep-water walleye renaissance. Lake Erie anglers cannot claim full credit for the rediscovery of walleye fishing in Erie waters. This rebirth came as a result of the import of equipment and techniques first applied in taking salmonids from Lake Ontario.

In the late 1970's, a few charter captains from Lake Michigan and Lake Ontario first brought downriggers and later planer boards on Lake Erie and tried salmon spoons and plugs at suspended levels. Rig trollers on those other two lakes had already experienced a decade of successes with salmon and trout cruising at depths well above the lake's bottom, and these rigs were designed to simulate errant bait schools moving in front of these suspended trout and salmon.

Commercial netters had known for decades that walleye in Lake Erie, like salmonids in other Great Lakes, often could be taken in great numbers at depths well above the bottom. Early in the warm-water season, many nets were set just a few feet below the surface over depths of 50 feet and more. There will be much more about this phenomenon later in the book.

The conventional wisdom among sport fishermen had long been that the walleye was exclusively a bottom-relating fish. The results of the application of modern techniques proved otherwise. In a relatively short time, suspended-walleye fishing with rigs and boards became so popular that large numbers of rig fishermen began to queue at every major access site along the Erie shoreline.

The stocking of salmonids here also took many of its cues from Lakes Michigan and Ontario. Assorted species have been tried and many have fared well, including the native lake trout. After near extirpation by the predations of the sea lamprey and the effects of pollution, the laker is coming back. Controls of predators, restricted catch limits and restocking programs are gradually bringing forktails back to prominence. Each year, reports of greater sizes and numbers of lake trout come into the Lake Erie Fisheries Management Unit at Dunkirk, New York, by anglers fishing the deeper waters in the Eastern Basin of the lake.

Rainbows, steelhead and brown trout are now prospering in the tributaries and open waters of Lake Erie. Seasonal patterns and open-water forays of these trout draw large numbers of anglers to shoreline and navigable tributary sites at those times of the year free of ice.

Chinook (king) salmon and silver (coho) salmon add yet another dimension. Though not a match for the sizes reached in Lake Ontario waters, Erie can boast a stocking program that brings abundant salmon—particularly cohos—within reach of shoreline anglers on most major feeder streams along the entire New York shoreline. Many are also taken in Pennsylvania and Ohio waters.

Thick schools of high-protein forage—mainly rainbow smelt—feed not only the walleye but also the king salmon, which have increased in size each year. For example, the winning king salmon entries in the Lake Erie International tournament for the past three years have increased from the high teens in 1987 to a 25-pound king caught during the 1990 LEI.

The public image of Lake Erie, then, so long trod upon by the public and the media, has slowly brightened. With the restoration of cleaner waters, many happy fishermen are now catching a vast assortment of fish. And Lake Erie is once again assuming its rightful place as one of the great lakes of the world.

Dozens of individual access sites and major metropolitan areas with extensive fishing facilities exist along the shoreline of Lake Erie. The lake, however, is often seen as consisting of three general areas

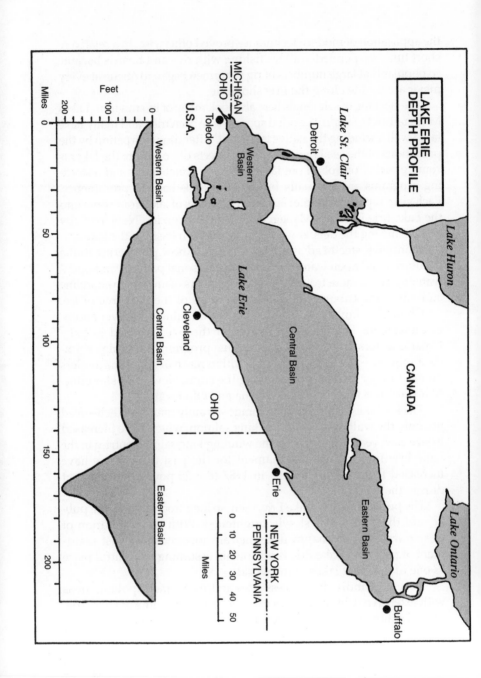

LAKE ERIE
DEPTH PROFILE

Lake St. Clair

Detroit

Lake Huron

MICHIGAN
OHIO

Toledo

U.S.A.

Western
Basin

Lake Erie

Central Basin

Cleveland

OHIO

CANADA

Erie

NEW YORK
PENNSYLVANIA

Eastern Basin

Lake Ontario

Buffalo

Miles
0   10 20 30 40 50
Miles

Feet
200
100
0

Miles
0   50   100   150   200

Western Basin   Central Basin   Eastern Basin

or basins: the Western Basin (Toledo-Port Clinton-Sandusky); the Central Basin (Lorain-Cleveland-Geneva-Conneaut-Ashtabula); and the Eastern Basin (Erie-Dunkirk-Buffalo).

Western Basin

Credit for the revival of Lake Erie must first go to the fishery that has emerged in the Western Basin. The relatively shallow water and vast system of access sites brought much regional and national attention to Erie. The draw was not facilities or tourist attractions; fishermen simply started hearing about massive schools of suspended walleye that were being located and caught. Consistent limit catches of walleye taken in a few short hours of fishing does much to popularize a fishery.

The state of Ohio was quick to realize that sport fishing offered a great potential for tourism. The fishery offered a renewable resource which could bring anglers into the state and out on its waters repeatedly. Ohio moved quickly in banning commercial fishing so that this sport fishery would not be jeopardized. The results seem to confirm that the banning of gill nets was a positive step in the developing and retaining of good fishing prospects year after year. Today, party and charter boats generate more income than the income once derived from commercial netting, and sport fishing revenues continue to increase.

Central Basin

This basin has just recently gained attention. While the Western Basin boasts great numbers of walleye and the Eastern Basin can flaunt its mixture of big walleye and assorted salmonids, the Central Basin offers up walleye in both size and numbers on a regular basis.

Starting in June and continuing until sometime in September, migrating schools of walleye in varying sizes concentrate around Ruggles Reef (east of Huron) and steadily move east as the summer progresses. A daily check is sometimes necessary as these fish move from Huron east to Lorain, Cleveland, Fairport/Painesville, Geneva and eventually the Ashtabula/Conneaut area. In some years it is entirely possible for the walleye schools to be heavy in many or all Central Basin areas at the same time. When the right combination of bait and favorable water conditions prevail, everyone has a banner year for walleye. Another recent development has been the number of "double figure" walleye that have been taken in the Central Basin. Once mainly exclusive to trollers in the Eastern Basin, many fish in the 10- to 12-pound range have been taken off Conneaut, Ashtabula and Geneva in recent years.

Eastern Basin

If an angler were to target trophy-sized walleye and good-sized salmonids, the deeper sections of the Eastern Basin would probably be the most likely area for successful outings. All areas of Lake Erie hold the potential for walleye in excess of ten pounds, but the deep waters of the Erie-to-Buffalo section offer the best odds.

Various species of salmon and trout (wild and stocked varieties) add another important dimension to the Eastern Basin. Trout and salmon take up residence in these same depths and often assume the same feeding patterns as the huge schools of walleye. Light tackle is still worth trying, but drag systems and line must be top quality and capable of handling fish that can empty a spool very quickly.

In short, there is not a "poor" or even an "only fair" fishing area on Lake Erie. At selected times of the warm-water season, Lake Erie offers more fishing alternatives than could be sampled by even those fortunate anglers with unlimited free time. Take a retired guy who has no family commitments, a wife who either fishes or loves house-work, kids who go off to college and need little money and a partner or two in the same circumstances. Even if this were one's lifestyle, Lake Erie would be too much to cover in one season on all fishing fronts.

Main Feeders

Major Erie tributaries vary in size and in the variety of species they offer, but they all have one thing in common: at varying times of the year they all hold sizeable schools of catchable walleye at their mouths and steelhead upstream.

With a current slightly less than the Niagara, the Detroit River supports a riverside fishery and influences walleye movements well out into the islands area of the Western Basin. Its outflow sometimes holds walleye schools in the open water of the Western

Basin long after they have left the shallows of reefs and shoals.

The Maumee River, wide and navigable with many rocky shallows, welcomes lines of casters just after ice-out each spring. Its spring walleye take often is a yardstick for conditions throughout the Western Basin when charter boats are finally able to get out and test the waters.

The Sandusky, Huron, Vermilion and Black Rivers all feature a large bay or area of protected water at their mouths. Trout and salmon runs occur each fall and good panfish numbers are recorded in the creel censuses taken along these rivers.

The Rocky, Cuyahoga and Chagrin Rivers—Cleveland-area feeders—share the dual features of heavy human populations near their mouths but remarkable trout fisheries upstream. Fly-casting purists and bait fishermen alike will find miles of undeveloped and unspoiled casting areas in which to fish for trout.

Grand River is the longest continual "trout stream" feeding into Lake Erie. The Grand, like the Cleveland and Ashtabula rivers, encompasses a two- to three-mile stretch of harbor water near the lake. Above Painesville, nearly 45 miles of stream await steelhead trout fishermen every season when the fish are in.

The Ashtabula River, like the Grand, has heavy industry at its mouth. Upstream, though, there are stretches of steep bluffs, wide oxbow turns, pools of varied depth and medium-gradient runoff. Conneaut Creek, approximately ten miles east of Ashtabula, courses through similar terrain and offers essentially the same kind of fishing. In places, the two feeders are less than two miles apart.

The Cattaraugus River, called Cattaraugus Creek by area anglers, is the only river-sized tributary flowing into Lake Erie in New York State. It supports a heavy run of both trout and salmon and has a broad system of feeder creeks suitable for fly fishing. It draws a mixed bag of warm-water species to its mouth and lower stretches each warm-weather season. Walleye, smallmouth, perch and even northern pike runs are common at certain times of the year.

Chapter 2

Fish and Fisheries Management: A Brief History

It's a calm summer night a year or two after World War II. A group of fishermen are sitting in their open boats and staring into their glowing propane lanterns. They look down into a gathering school of baitfish and collectively think that the blue pike could never be cleaned out of Lake Erie—ever. Only twenty years later, commercial netters would not be able to bring in a single specimen of this once superabundant subspecies of the walleye. Lake Erie has had its share of happy stories through the years, but we'll begin with one of the unhappiest.

Blue Pike: One Sad Fish

September 2, 1983: Certainly no July 4, 1776 or a day in 1066, 1492 or 1945. But that date marks a most important event in the history of Lake Erie in particular and fisheries management in general.

On September 2, 1983 the Director of the U.S. Fish and Wildlife Service officially declared the "blue pike" *(Stizostedion vitreum glaucum)* an extinct fish.

Long a controversial creature, this smaller cousin of the walleye was once abundant throughout Lake Erie and some adjacent waters. During the last century, catch reports for commercial gill-netters totaled approximately 990 tons. No figures could be accurately gathered for the tonnage of blue pike taken from Lake Erie by sport fishermen.

The blue pike was not officially identified as a separate species until 1926. In that year, Carl C. Hubbs did a "nomenclatural and analytical key," an identification procedure which showed this fish to be separate from all other species. Ten years later he reentered the fish as a subspecies of the walleye—rather than as a distinct species of fish.

By 1957 it was becoming difficult to catch "blues" in Lake Erie with either hook and line or commercial nets. The last blues reported taken by commercial nets was in 1965.

No one cause can be singled out for the decline and eventual disappearance of this once dominant food fish in Lake Erie. Perhaps it is a combination of all of the following:

POLLUTION/OXYGEN DEPLETION. Increasing amounts of both chemical and organic wastes were dumped into the lake's waters with the population movement to Erie's shores following World War II. As the pollutants increased, oxygen was reduced in the cooler waters preferred by blue pike.

COMPETITION WITH EXOTIC SPECIES. In the late 1950's after the opening of the St. Lawrence Seaway, many new species of fish appeared in Lake Erie. Some were freshwater species and some were species that lived (or could live) alternately in salt and fresh water. Of the many invaders that took hold in the Great Lakes, the most enduring was the rainbow smelt. While beneficial to many species, the smelt came into direct competition with the blue pike for its food supply and also threatened the survival of their offspring. Smelt feed on the same bug life that supported blue pike. Smelt also fed on the eggs and fry hatches of blue pike.

SELECTIVE FISHING. Few or no regulations were imposed on commercial and sport fishermen. There was an indifference to the initial declining numbers of blue pike in the early '50's. No one considered them vulnerable. Observers were well aware that their numbers took radical swings downward only to rebound after a year or two. Since there were no formal studies of blue pike behavior, restocking programs could not be quickly established when the depth of the downslide became obvious.

INTROGRESSIVE HYBRIDIZATION. An elaborate term for repeated crossbreedings. As the blues declined, it seemed apparent that they were crossbreeding with the walleyes to the extent that blue-colored walleyes were entering into the fishery. Many observers assumed these crossbreeds were true blues. Another false hope emerged when grey-colored walleye began to appear. But these off-colored walleye never reproduced an offspring which could be identified as blue pike.

By the time a Blue Pike Recovery Plan was formulated and a team of noted fisheries biologists was brought together in 1975, the fish was too far gone. Only non-reproducing older specimens could be found. It is suspected that the "blues" the team were finding were actually crossbreeds, showing blue coloration but reproducing walleye rather than blue pike offspring. In just a few years of study it was confirmed that the fish was no longer able to be produced—in hatcheries or naturally.

Samples of off-colored walleye were found in some lakes in the Province of Ontario (Ontario biologists referred to them as "blue walleye"), but the offspring of these fish in all breeding attempts turned out to be "yellow pike" (i.e. walleye).

The blue pike is gone. Many people still cherish fond memories of this abundant food fish which was caught by the boat load under lantern lights that shone from the gunwales of thousands of boats all along the Erie shoreline. Here is a sample of some of the anecdotal reports gathered by the "Blue Pike Recovery Team" and from recollections of Lake Erie area anglers who had fished for blues in years past:

> *"Round-bottom boats had to be unloaded in shallow water at Sturgeon Point before the boat could be beached for fear of swamping the vessel as it was being pulled onto shore. The cause: Excessive amounts of blue pike on board which were*

sinking the craft and making it impossible to pull onto the beach."

"Catches of blues in 1923 were so great that one writer noted the market was 'going soft' because of the heavy volume of fillets supplied from Lake Erie processors."

"Just after World War II, lantern lights on Lake Erie formed what appeared to be a continuous light—two to six miles from shore—stretching from Buffalo to well past Dunkirk Harbor. Farther west, the long white line continued past Erie, Pennsylvania and often beyond Cleveland."

"Boaters had to motor at trolling speeds for a mile or more through anchored boats off Point Breeze in the Town of Evans before finding an opening wide enough between other boats to drop anchor and have room to make short casts from either side of their boats."

"Casters working the breakwaters along the shoreline of the upper Niagara River needed only a large pearl fixed above an unbaited hook once the blues began moving close to shore sometime shortly after sunset."

"A Cleveland commentator in 1940 remarked that blue pike fishing should be considered a 'food fishery' rather than a 'sport fishery' because of the tons of fish caught by both commercial and sport fishermen."

"As late as 1950, blue pike fishing supported nightly trips for 25 party boats—with carrying capacities ranging from 20 to 60 anglers—from Erie, Pennsylvania. Parties would leave in shifts and quite often fill the boat with more than enough blues for everyone on board in a few short hours of fishing."

"Friday 'fish specials' in Western New York restaurants were universally blue pike dinners. Sales of chicken wings and beef-on-weck together could not match the number of blue pike that crossed the

dinner plate each Friday night. Blue pike fillets once sold at Dunkirk Pier for 14 cents a pound, and area restaurants could easily put together a 'blue pike special' (dinner with all the trimmings) for less than a dollar a plate."

The disappearance of the blue pike in Lake Erie was a great loss. It hammers home the point that even a superabundant species can be wiped out with amazing speed. But fisheries management has come a long way in the past few decades. At the same time, sport fishermen today are often the first to stand up to protect a declining species. We have learned to observe changes in fishery conditions and manage them in a way that fishing conditions improve rather than decline.

Popular Species
As mentioned earlier, the walleye must be credited with bringing new attention to fishing in Lake Erie, since the fish's rediscovery in the Western Basin in the mid-1970's. Now found and consistently caught in all parts of the lake, the walleye is the most universally sought game fish on Lake Erie. A stop at any bait and tackle shop along the lake bears this out, since in-stock tackle items are heavily keyed to walleye fishing. Also, the people who frequent these shops predominately fish for walleye.

While the walleye gets a stronger nod from fishermen, the most consistently available species has to be the bass—the smallmouth bass. Largemouth bass can be found in bays and in some open waters at times, but smallmouths are the more dominant. These fish can be found in tributaries, bays, embayments and in open waters several miles from shore at any depth which holds large schools of bait.

Once the only major panfish popular with anglers here, the yellow perch now shares the limelight with white perch, white bass, rock bass and even the lowly sheepshead. Caught in shallows along the shoreline and on the bottom out in the shipping lanes from Toledo to Buffalo, the perch probably has caused more anchors to be sent to the bottom of Lake Erie than all other catchable species of fish combined. Associated primarily with the spring and fall seasons, perch can sometimes be caught on any fishable day of any season of the year. Only fickle bait movements and bad weather conditions slow the perch-seeking bucket brigade on Lake Erie.

Native to Lake Erie but seriously depleted by sea lamprey predation, the lake trout might be considered the species best symbolizing the comeback of Lake Erie. Lakers are taken in Ohio waters, but the larger schools hold in the cooler, deeper waters off Pennsylvania and New York. Anglers (mainly trollers) often specifically target these fish with deep-set lines at depths which show fish activity on the sonar screen. No other salmonid species is specifically targeted here with this deep-water tackle. Its fight can hardly match the battle put forth by a muskellunge or king salmon, but a lake trout taken on a medium-light trolling rod can keep someone busy at the transom for quite a while. Its fight leaves many a walleye troller impressed and exhausted.

Stocked in varying numbers by all four states which border Lake Erie, rainbow and steelhead trout are intentionally fished for in many of Erie's principal feeder streams and rivers. Steelies show up among walleye schools in every section of the lake, but most of those taken in open water are caught incidentally. It's when the steelhead move into tributaries that anglers set out specifically to catch them. With the introduction of a new steelhead strain called "skamania," trout fishing in the streams may become a nearly year-long thing. Skamania are more tolerant of warmer waters than other trout and will enter and hold in rivers and streams outside the traditional steelhead season.

Two kinds of salmon are stocked in Lake Erie: chinook and coho. Most hatcheries provide greater numbers of coho than king salmon, but it is the larger king that reigns supreme and makes for the best picture-taking and story-telling. In 1989, for example, much media hoopla ensued when Red Shumacher of Ashtabula brought in a 29.5-pound king salmon to break the Ohio state record for that species, a record which had stood for 17 years. Curiously, the State of Ohio does not even stock king salmon in Lake Erie. This fish probably had been stocked in either Pennsylvania or New York State. The more numerous and catchable salmon species is the coho, which fisheries biologists consider more adaptable to Lake Erie's waters. Usually weighing in at less than 10 pounds here, the unpredictable fight of these silver scrappers makes them a most exciting sport fishing addition. Although these two Pacific salmon usually return to the streams in which they were originally stocked, successful natural reproduction of these fish in Erie tributaries is minuscule if not nil. We must rely on stocking to continue this exciting salmon fishery.

Muskellunge and northern pike, two larger members of the *Esox* genus, are not widely distributed in Lake Erie. The mecca of musky fishing in Erie waters is the upper Niagara River, the outflow of Lake Erie at Buffalo. Many muskies exceeding 20 pounds are caught each season in the Niagara River and in the Buffalo Harbor area called "the head of the river." Northern pike are found in modest numbers in Huron Bay, Sandusky Bay and the Presque Isle Bay area in Erie, Pennsylvania. Tourism bureaus, however, do not usually hype these species, or use them to attempt to draw anglers from faraway places. The fishing for pike and muskies in Lake Erie is exciting but limited, except in the Niagara River.

All other catchable species might be considered panfish, although there are other species that some still call trash fish. Included here would be suckers, carp, bullhead, catfish and sheepshead. Before the ban on gill netting in Ohio and New York, catch rates for sheepshead were declining steadily. All fisheries agencies today consider these species "manageable" and institute no programs for their removal.

White bass and white perch are late arrivals in the catch count of fishermen. Though some anglers specifically go out to find these species, they usually show up as incidental catches by fishermen seeking yellow perch.

Catch-Up Fisheries Management

Observations in retrospect make everyone seem wise. We now know that the fishery problems Lake Erie suffered in the past were caused by us all and must be understood and resolved by all of us.

It would appear that state and federal agencies were slow in getting together plans to clean up Erie's waters and restore the immense sport fishing potential of this fertile lake. In fact, hundreds of competent fisheries personnel had been actively studying and carefully outlining conditions and changes in Lake Erie and other Great Lakes in reports—some published before the Civil War.

But it was not until public awareness heightened that the scientific people could put their data to work. Then, monies were spent on more comprehensive studies of water quality, environmentally sound laws were passed to decrease—if not eliminate—continued pollution, and people again began to look at Lake Erie as an exciting place to go fishing.

Between 1970 and 1990 Lake Erie's water quality and sport fishing improved beyond any projection that could have been made in the 1960's.

Water quality in Lake Erie, though still far from ideal, is such that native fish, stocked species and "ballast bums"—salt- and fresh-water aquatic life forms introduced to Great Lakes waters during indiscriminate discharge of ballast waters—are all thriving and have generally increased in numbers in the past two decades.

Of the several large game fish native to Lake Erie, the most popular species are walleye, smallmouth bass and lake trout. Survival rates for these three species varied during the period 1970-1990. Walleye oscillated, declining seriously in near-shore areas. Then they staged a comeback in the 1970's from the deep–water areas where they suspended. Lake trout, the dominant salmonoid species in Lake Erie's aquatic history, nearly disappeared, but a substantial recovery occurred through the 1980's.

Fisheries studies indicate that natural yearly walleye production can vary by more than 10 million fish per year. In New York, for example, the 1983 year class was virtually nonexistent. The '84 class numbered almost 12 million and the '85 class fell just below two million, according to estimates. Collective figures for the entire lake generally place the holding population of walleye anywhere between 20 and 60 million fish. Natural walleye production much depends upon weather conditions during and after the walleye egg-hatching period. One lengthy storm, washing huge, silting waves against Lake Erie's open shoreline, and an entire year class of walleye may be destroyed.

Bass have remained stable. Anyone who can cast from shore or rent or borrow a small boat can find smallmouth black bass somewhere near

*Fish are the golden fleece for the research vessel **Argo**, here asail on the waters off Dunkirk Harbor. The **Argo** will routinely travel from Buffalo to Barcelona in search of data which will help to better manage fisheries in Lake Erie's Eastern Basin.*

the shoreline during the warmer months of the year. Bass have continually survived predation from larger species and the many pollutants placed in their waters. While biologists have established regulations to protect bass, there has never been a need to raise bass in hatcheries for stocking here. The greater concerns have been a) to protect the bass's habitat, and b) control the amount of "hooking mortality." If too many fish are caught and released with fatal hook damage, there may be a problem even when catch-and-release is widely practiced.

In fact, it may be that bass fishermen are getting too good at their sport. That is, at certain times of the fishing season experienced fishermen might possibly overharvest the larger breeding smallmouths, leaving smaller fish that may only reproduce smaller strains of smallmouth bass.

Fisheries management agencies in Michigan, Ohio, Pennsylvania and New York all have established protective seasons and creel limits to avoid the possibility that bass might be injured or killed by too many hooks.

Pennsylvania, for example, has enacted a series of regulations for bass fishing which will take force in 1991: The length limit is increased from 12 to 15 inches, the creel limit during the open season is reduced from six to four fish, and the creel limit during spawning season (formerly two fish) has been eliminated. Check fishing regulations for specific dates and area stipulations. Sportsmen almost unanimously supported these protective changes in order to assure a continued sport fishery which will include larger fish in catchable numbers.

This lake trout, taken from the deep waters off Barcelona Harbor, hit a spoon run off a downrigger set at 140 feet. The lake is once again clean enough to support this great char of the depths, but at present most fish taken are from stockings. A natural population of lakers once existed in Lake Erie.

Lake trout can be a management maze. They are native to Lake Erie waters and, in the past, thrived in the deeper waters of the east and central basins of the lake. Predation from sea lampreys has reduced their numbers, despite more than a quarter century of lampricide treatments at lamprey spawning sites. Lake trout, unlike salmon, live for decades and require a steady, high-protein forage base. They can feed as heavily during a warm winter as they do during the other seasons. At least some natural reproduction appears to be occurring in Erie, though officials are slow to confirm this.

New York State has imposed a one-fish limit on lake trout in Lake Erie waters and has established a division in its Lake Erie Unit at Dunkirk devoted specifically to studying and improving the lake trout fishery. Biologists at Dunkirk have been working on every aspect of lake trout management, from enumeration studies to planting of hatchery fish in the deep, cold water preferred by these fish. The future of the native lake trout is not completely clear, but the species is being carefully observed and nurtured.

Walleye management presents more problems than solutions. In principle, a walleye fishery could continue with only one successful year-class every five years, according to John Anderson, former fisheries manager with the U.S. Fish and Wildlife station at Warren, Pa. Anderson successfully introduced walleye to Pennsylvania's Kinzua Reservoir, partially by augmenting the lake's forage base through the introduction of rainbow smelt.

Stocking walleye and developing a fishery for them in a much larger body of water like Lake Erie is yet another matter. For years, the S.O.N.S. of Lake Erie (an acronym for Save Our Native Species) have managed a walleye fry rearing operation at Erie, with the cooperation of the Pennsylvania Fish Commission. Each year, volunteers raise walleye from the egg stage up to past the critical "eye fry" stage so that they can be planted in the somewhat protected waters of Presque Isle Bay. Fry numbers vary from year to year; mortality just after hatching can occur with just a few degrees of change in the water temperature at critical periods. But the S.O.N.S. have faithfully planted fry each year for almost a decade.

Results of walleye stocking cannot yet be determined. Though optimistic about the project, Sheryl Hood, Director of the Linesville Hatchery, cannot show proof that a single adult walleye has resulted from these hatchery efforts. Scale coding techniques in the future may prove that hatchery walleye have made it to maturity. But for now, fishery studies indicate that wild, naturally produced walleyes make up the main population of fish we have and catch in Lake Erie.

With the elimination of gill netting in Ohio and New York State, many fishery studies have been made more complex. Today, fishery managers cannot simply check with a few good captains and put together reasonable figures on fish populations and trends. Although there are other sources, state officials have had to rely largely upon a sport fishing and charter boat creel census.

One interesting statistic comes from "Status and Trend Highlights: Ohio's Fish and Fisheries." The estimated 1989 total fish harvest was an impressive 18.2 million pounds— an above-average but not record total for a year. The remarkable part is the breakdown of the catch: charter boats took 14% and commercial netting accounted for 26%, but fully 60 percent of the catch was taken by private boats. In sum, everyday sport fishermen are catching more than half of the fish in Ohio waters. From all appearances, approximately the same percentages apply in the waters of the other Lake Erie states. Pennsylvania, with closely supervised netting quotas, sees much more sport fishing activity than either charter or commercial fishing activity.

What is the future of Lake Erie? The answer is a qualified "excellent." No agency or species-oriented group can guarantee that any kind of fish will continue to thrive in a lake as big and diverse as Lake Erie. However, fishery reports and the attendant awareness of an interested fishing public have made problems easier to identify; it's now more possible than ever to solve them before they become critical.

Immediately following the inaugural Earth Day on April 22, 1970, there went forth a widely publicized mandate to clean up the United States waters of Lake Erie. That wasn't the first "beginning."

Certain scientists had been well aware of and attempting to deal with Lake Erie's many pollution problems for decades. Henry A. Regier, in the Great Lakes Fishery Commission publication *The Ecol-*

ogy and Management of the Walleye In Lake Erie (Technical Report # 15 May, 1969) wrote:

"We are optimistic about the intensified pollution abatement programs currently in effect on Lake Erie. The view propagated by some persons that once a lake becomes polluted it is 'dead' is simply wrong. Lakes can recover, and the Western Basin of Lake Erie might recover rather rapidly under intelligent management."

The wisdom of these words was borne out less than a decade later when miles-long schools of suspended walleye began to appear in the Western Basin and fishermen started developing tackle and techniques specifically designed to hook into these fish.

The New York State Conservation Department became the Department of Environmental Conservation, opening its doors on July 1, 1970. This department, along with the Fish Commission of The Commonwealth of Pennsylvania, and the Department of Natural Resources of both Ohio and Michigan, immediately began looking and relooking at ways to prevent all forms of environmentally unsafe substances from entering the waters of Lake Erie.

Through the 1970's, these four state agencies began a rigorous program to upgrade water quality and create conditions whereby the public could once again reap the benefits of Lake Erie. Hatcheries, mainly devoted to the rearing of salmonids, were built and/or expanded. The impressive Linesville Hatchery in northwestern Pennsylvania, for example, opened new pond areas and expanded its public access/exhibit capability. Today, a fisherman and his family could share an enjoyable day viewing the many facilities open to visitors at the Linesville Hatchery.

No single group has been exclusively responsible for the restored beauty of this bounteous inland sea. It has taken the collective efforts of many people in politics, governmental fisheries bureaus, water-dependent industries, public utility companies, area residents and Lake Erie fishermen. All these men and women deserve high regard for their labors, often given freely and without compensation.

Chapter 3

Charter Chatter and Ports of Call

There are essentially four different ways to fish Lake Erie: From shore, from a private boat, from a charter boat and from a head boat. In this chapter we will look at charter and head boat fishing, and then list the important ports around Lake Erie where you can hook up with both types of fishing vessels.

But first, what is the difference? For those who might not know, here is a brief description.

A charter boat is usually hired or "chartered" privately. On Erie, these boats average about 30 feet in length and take an average of three to six passengers. Three to four is about the norm. The passengers are given a lot of attention by both the captain and the mate (there is almost always a mate on board) and the price reflects this. A half-day charter averages $175 on Lake Erie while a full-day charter averages $275. These prices vary, but one way or the other a charter boat patron can expect to pay from $60 to $150 depending on the boat and number on board.

A typical chartering license for trollers is called a "six pack," which provides for up to six chartered passengers per vessel. Few boats are large enough to accommodate more than twelve lines (in states allowing two lines per person) while trolling.

Head boats, as they are most often called here, are the inland equivalent of the ever popular party boats operating along the Atlantic coast. They're open to the public, although sometimes a group will "charter" an entire party boat for the day...say for an office outing or a club event. Head boats on Erie average 40 feet in length and can carry—when full—an average of 20 passengers. Just show up in the morning, or at the advertised sailing time, pay your money, and let the experienced captain and crew take you to the fishing grounds.

At present there are approximately 1,200 charter boats operating on Lake Erie, many of them part-time operations. There are presently about 700 head boats. These are usually full-time, although seasonal, enterprises.

The Charter Game

A well-planned charter may start a year in advance, since booking a particular date may be important to you. At the least, the arrangements should be made several months in advance.

An excellent way to find charter boats is at the big outdoor shows held in arenas and convention centers, normally during the winter and early spring months. Stroll through the aisles and you'll come across the booths of many charter boats, and probably even get to meet some captains. Usually, you can pick a date, pay a deposit and book your charter right on the spot. Before you do, though, study the brochure the captain gives you, and determine whether the captain and crew seem affable and competent. If the chemistry seems wrong, go visit some other booths before plopping down your money. And never be afraid to ask questions.

David O. Kelch, District Extension Specialist with the Ohio Sea Grant, has put together a series of questions that should be asked before making a charter choice.

Ask about cost, including the amount of deposit and the total cost of the trip. Be sure that you fully understand all costs before you make any commitment.

Find out exactly when the day begins and ends. This can vary widely.

Know what the provisions are in the event of a cancellation. Many things can occur: foul weather, no acceptable alternate booking dates in the event of a postponement, personal problems on either side, and last-minute events which cause you to arrive late at the dock. Know the terms of refunding in advance. Do you get your deposit back if a cancellation becomes necessary?

Duration of the trip is yet another important consideration. Ask whether the charter will be for a set number of hours afloat or just to the point at which all clients have caught a limit of fish. Kelch writes, "If your party limits within a few hours, other species may be pursued in the remaining time (perch, white bass, smallmouth bass, freshwater drum). Or, you may want to take a leisurely cruise around the islands or to Put-In-Bay, or you may wish to anchor in calm waters for a swim." But if these terms are not established beforehand, your captain may head back to port once a limit of fish (typically walleyes) is taken by all clients.

Find out if there are additional charges when extra time is spent during the charter. In the event the trip requires greater running time or unscheduled side trips for any reason, find out what fees the captain would charge.

Before going out with a particular charter boat for the first time—even if you are a veteran, familiar with the type of fishing done aboard these boats—ask what you should bring. Ask if you must bring your own tackle (rods, reels, lures, etc.) or if they will be supplied by the charter. Ask if ice is included or not. If these items are supplied, are they included in the total cost as they usually are, or are they additional? When live bait is used, ask if it is supplied. If it's not, and you have to bring it, ask how much is enough for the hours to be spent afloat.

Especially during the warm summer months, cooler space is essential. Find out if space is provided for lunches as well as the catch. If not, you may wish to bring a small cooler for lunch and drinks (almost never supplied by the boat).

Ask about the crew and the boat itself. Find out if, in fact, this boat has all the proper licenses to operate as a fishing charter boat. Check to see that all the required safety equipment is in place. Don't be embarrassed to ask about toilet facilities. This is mandatory equipment for a charter vessel.

In spite of many of the above suggestions, understand that charter boats supply most or all of the fishing equipment on most trips. And, because they usually troll rather than drift or anchor, live bait is rarely needed.

What The Captain Expects From You

You're paying good money for your charter and you'll expect a lot from your captain. There are also a few things he'll expect of you.

Go through your equipment and consolidate it, taking aboard only what's necessary for the trip at hand. This includes fishing tackle. If you are bringing your own gear, check for faulty knots and weak (old or frayed) line. Do all this a night or two before the trip begins, so you'll have time to do what's necessary.

Take precautions for motion sickness, if that's normally a problem for you. Check with your doctor. Some "seasick" remedies may cause drowsiness or aggravate a health condition in conflict with other medications. As always, avoid greasy foods and alcohol the night before the trip.

Be on time. Your promptness will allow the captain and crew to concentrate on their immediate tasks of setting up the boat and the equipment without worrying whether their clients will show or not. An early arrival—particularly on your first outing—will allow you to look over equipment, ask a few additional questions that may not have been posed in earlier conversations, and get a feel for how this charter boat will approach the day's fishing and weather conditions. Arriving early gives you the chance to think things through, and make sure you've taken from the car everything you wanted to bring on the boat.

Needless to say, never—under any circumstances—throw trash overboard. Trash containers are kept aboard all chartering vessels so that paper, cans, old line, and other refuse items do not litter Lake Erie.

One last item of utmost concern: alcoholic beverages. Most charter captains have policies on drinking and usually draw the line at a beer or two with no hard liquor on board. Ship rules vary, but the main concern is safety for all. Many captains will tell all passengers before the vessel leaves port that excessive drinking will result in suspension of the trip and the vessel will return to port with no refunds. Ohio watercraft regulations prohibit any person on a boat from being under the influence and other states are now enforcing laws against vessel operators driving while impaired. The problem with one or more impaired persons is that all on board are suddenly forced into the unwelcome role of brother's keeper. In rough weather, in particular, this could distract a captain who has to concentrate on safety considerations. The best advice is to skip the alcohol completely. Bring a few sodas and sandwiches, and enjoy your day on the water.

Head Boats and Head Boaters

Taking their cue from the vast fleet of saltwater party boats on the Atlantic and Pacific seaboards, many enterprising individuals have established businesses to harvest Erie's new found bounties. Currently, most Erie party boats operate in the Western Basin. They charge per head as anglers walk on daily and, technique-wise, usually either drift or anchor.

A typical head boat outing requires that you bring the following: suitable clothing, deck or other non-slip shoes, a small cooler for lunch and drinks (and, hopefully, for carrying fish fillets on the way home), sunblock in summer, sunglasses and whatever bait and tackle items you might need. These will vary considerably and must be investigated ahead of time.

The captain or deck hand will willingly share with you information about previous or recent trips, and explain the approach to be taken on this trip. It's important to listen up as the boat heads out so you can set up your rod, rigs and baits in the manner suggested. When the engine idles down and the "all fish" signal is sounded, every patron should be ready to fish; and each should have an equal chance of catching fish. Party boat fishing is quite relaxing since the captain does all the work and is responsible for finding the fish.

Deck hands keep an accurate count of the fish each angler has taken and placed on ice. Most hands will take your fish and immediately place them on numbered stringers in the main cooler. "Big fish" and "most unusual" contests can be entered for a few bucks, usually collected by the deck hands. This is always optional, and always separate from the fee for boarding the boat.

Most head boats charge an average of $20 per day. Rental equipment is commonly available, and costs a few bucks extra. Any fees for bait or lost equipment items are a matter of policy of the particular boat or trip.

Another option is the cleaning and packaging of fish at the end of the trip. Many head boats, like the ocean operations, have efficient hands who will clean your fish for a modest fee. Ports with even a small fleet of head boats have at least one fish cleaning establishment somewhere at or near the docking area. On the other hand, some states do not allow fish to be cleaned aboard boats or at dockside. Check the regulations for the state in which you are fishing.

At the beginning of this chapter, we named the four primary

The largest party boat currently operating on Lake Erie, the 72-foot **Miss Majestic,** *being readied for another run. Its area of concentration: The perch and walleye grounds in the Central Basin waters off of Lorain.*

ways of fishing Lake Erie. There is actually a fifth way: going out in a rental skiff. Regrettably, the rental livery business has greatly shrunk on Erie. Some people ascribe their demise to dramatically increased insurance premiums. Others say they succumbed during Erie's "dead years". Still others say that today's greater affluence did in the rental fleets—more people than ever before can now afford their own boats. Whatever the reasons, rental boat liveries are all but gone from the back bays and coves of the shoreline along which they once thrived. No more than about 10 boat liveries currently exist along Erie's U.S. shoreline, and more than half of these require customers to bring their own outboard motors.

In the next chapter, we'll look at some important considerations for tackling Lake Erie's blossoming fishing in your own craft. One more thought, though, is worth passing on here.

If you will be fishing mainly out of a private boat, yours or a friend's, you can learn much by going out on a charter or party boat from time to time. The captain knows the waters better than you ever will—that's his profession. On one trip, you should pick up enough good tips to last you a long while. You may even find the experience suits you so well that thoughts of buying your own rig will fade away. A great many anglers only have time to get out three or four times a year, in spite of intentions to the contrary. That's why thousands of boats in America sit on front lawns with "For Sale" signs propped up on the windshields.

Consider the following example: In one year, one angler could go out on five charters and, taking into consideration a minimal expenditure on tackle, have less than $600 invested in fishing for that year. By contrast, a new boat-and-trailer rig might cost somewhere around $10,000. Even with a large down payment, installments can be as great as on a car. But with a boat, the initial cost is only the beginning. Maintenance fees, fuel, accessories, storage, motor repairs—the list of supplementary costs goes on and on.

A private boat that can realistically deal with the big waters of Lake Erie is a big investment any way you plan it. For many people, charter and head boat fishing is a better alternative.

Although there are more head boats in the Western Basin, both head boats and charter boats are available all along the U.S. shoreline of Lake Erie. What follows is an annotated list of those ports or locations where you can expect to find a for-hire boat that will suit your needs.

Michigan

MONROE. Though overshadowed in numbers by Ohio's fishing fleet and greater water area, several boats run from Bolles Harbor.

Ohio

TOLEDO. Off the lake but well attached to the waterway, Toledo is a short ride down the Maumee River to the westernmost areas of the Western Basin. Call the Greater Toledo Office of Tourism and Conventions.

PORT CLINTON. The most popular fishing site in the Western Basin. The name is synonymous with weight-forward spinners for walleye. Either the Port Clinton Chamber of Commerce or the Ottawa County Visitors Bureau can outline the many fishing possibilities this famed port has to offer.

SANDUSKY. Developing a walk-on fleet of head boats to complement its charter boat fleet, Sandusky is at the juncture of islands fishing to the west and the open-water stretches which bound the west end of the Central Basin. Detailed information can be gathered from the Erie County Visitors and Convention Bureau.

VEMILION-HURON. Bounded by giants in fishing options (Sandusky and Lorain), these two ports boast a good harbor, several chartering choices and an offshore fishery of both structure and suspended-depth fishing.

LORAIN. Harbor facilities include two large launch sites and more than 100 chartering choices at the newly completed Marina International. Lorain offers every fishing possibility available in Ohio's Central Basin. Call the Lorain County Visitor's Bureau.

CLEVELAND. A city which has come a long way since serving as the butt of gags on "Laugh-In" in the early 70's. Head boats, charter boats, and seven public launch sites exist within the city limits, affirming the popularity of fishing in this large, industrial city. Much can be learned with a call to the Convention and Visitors Bureau of Greater Cleveland.

FAIRPORT/PAINESVILLE. This area is dotted with smaller launch sites and offers fishing that is varied and full of surprises. Seasonal patterns make for an interesting mix of walleye and perch fishing which begins at different times each warm-weather season. Area launch sites and marina operations can also be found at Mentor-on-the-Lake and along the banks of the Grand River well into Painesville. Lake County Visitors Bureau can assist in helping you to learn more about this area.

GENEVA-ON-THE-LAKE. A state-operated marina with more than 350 slips available and six launch ramps (free to the public) make access to the good fishing in northeastern Ohio waters simple and quick. Three separate park areas on Lake Erie's shore offer combined fishing and other recreational activities: swimming, tennis, picnicking, etc. Handicapped fishermen have easy access to the water from a convenient pier facility at Geneva State Park.

ASHTABULA. An industrial city with the heart of a fisherman. Like the Grand River, the Ashtabula River banks are dotted with marinas and launching facilities. Ashtabula has developed the image of a "clean industrial" harbor where commerce and sport fishing both thrive. Detailed fishing information can be obtained from the Ashtabula County Planning Commission.

CONNEAUT. Vying with Ashtabula for fishing supremacy in the area, Conneaut offers the same basic fishing conditions. The shoreline structures and long, gradual drop-offs out to Canadian waters make these two ports nearly indistinguishable to someone out on the lake. Ask about each area when contacting the Ashtabula County Planning Commission and get set for some remarkable walleye fishing out of either one of these ports.

Pennsylvania

ERIE. With only three boat-launching access sites maintained by the state in or near the only city on Lake Erie's Pennsylvania shoreline, Erie offers a surprising number of fishing options for both the boating and shorebound angler. Boaters may access at either Presque Isle State Park (three separate ramps into Presque Isle Bay) and Northeast Access Area (two ramps into Presque Isle Bay and two ramps into Lake Erie). Five miles west of Erie, the Pennsylvania Fish

Commission maintains the Walnut Creek Access Area at the mouth of that creek (north of Route 5).

SAFE HARBOR MARINA. With dockage, boat storage and two launch ramps, this single facility is the only public access and docking site between Erie and Barcelona. Located in North East, this modest-but-functional operation may serve as a model for future fishing access sites on Lake Erie. Fishing and boating conditions for the Pennsylvania waters of Lake Erie are reported on the Fish Commission's hotline.

New York

BARCELONA/DUNKIRK. Two safe-water harbors with docking and launching facilities protected by breakwaters. For details on

N.Y. POWER AUTHORITY

Dunkirk Harbor. Most winters find the harbor surrounded with ice, but that was not the case here. A warm water discharge from the power plant shown can attract trout and salmon all winter long. Walleye, bass and panfish take over when the waters warm later in the season.

these popular Western New York fishing sites, contact the Chautauqua County Visitors Bureau.

CATTARAUGUS CREEK. The largest tributary in New York State has a state-operated launch plus two private launch sites and numerous docking sites.

STURGEON POINT. Recently expanded and upgraded, Sturgeon Point is a major access to Lake Erie's shallow- and deep-water fishing options. Sturgeon is the only major public access between Cattaraugus and the City of Buffalo.

BUFFALO. The city provides four public launch sites, largest of which is the Small Boat Harbor. Every prominent species of fish in Erie can now be found here at the extreme eastern end of the Eastern Basin. Call or write the Buffalo Area Visitors and Convention Center.

Chapter 4

Erie, One on One

The preceding chapter should have made clear the options you have for fishing Lake Erie itself (Part III will cover the tributaries). While charter boats and head boats can be not only sensible but rewarding, it is a fact that most Erie anglers will fish out of private boats.

Most of Part II is aimed at helping private boaters put more fish in their coolers (or at least on their lines, if they plan to release most). What follows here is intended to provide preliminary information for taking on this big lake one on one. Much of it is related to safety. A great lake is no place to learn basic seamanship. If you're new to private boating, approach her waters slowly and thoughtfully and she will pay you handsome rewards. Rush right out without forethought or planning and you could pay a dear price.

On any large body of water your vessel is your ultimate life preserver. Without an adequate one, you're "sunk" as far as successful fishing goes, and maybe literally as well.

The weather reigns on Lake Erie, and you might say, on all the Great Lakes. High winds can put a previously nice day on the rocks in minutes, and when this happens, shelter can sometimes be found in the lee of a manmade breakwater.

What Is a Safe Boat?

The U.S. Coast Guard recommends that Lake Erie boats smaller than 18 feet should stay close to shore. Those who routinely fish far offshore are better equipped with a boat 20 feet or longer. In the many protected bays and near-shore areas, 14 to 16-foot outboards can be and are used effectively. These close-to-shore small boaters seldom get into trouble until they decide to "test" the lake on what looks like a nice day. Nice days turn sour very fast here, however.

Whatever boat you choose, select a deep draft or "deep-vee" model with high sides and the ability to cut through chop. Flat-bottomed boats and "semi-vees" are much less desirable on big waters like Erie.

Just as important for safety is what you carry on board the boat. There are specific coast guard requirements, but they vary depending on the length of the craft. First of all, then, study coast guard regulations if you're fairly new to private boating. You'll be staying within the law at the same time you learn much about safety equipment and procedures. Approved life jackets, life buoys and flares may be among the more essential safety items. It's quite likely, though, that there are items a new seaman might not think of. By the way, just as important as having the right equipment is keeping it serviceable or in proper working order.

The Weather: Expect It To Change

Experienced boater-anglers on Lake Erie—those who have fished both large and small bodies of water with some frequency—generally agree that weather-related changes occur faster here and with more potential for destruction than on most other lakes.

Looking at a topographical map of the entire Great Lakes Chain, one notices that Lake Erie juts out into a varied mix of mountains and plains along its southern shoreline. Mixes of warm and cold air masses generate storm fronts which move over relatively shallow waters that kick up waves with close swells and crossing breezes which are difficult to ride out. During the winter months, the eastern half (Cleveland to Buffalo) experiences more average snowfall than the adjacent plains area as a result of prevailing winds moving directly up the full length of the lake (roughly west to east), creating what is known as lake effect snowfall. This can create a "white-out" that can make navigation back to port or movement on ice extremely difficult.

On-board safety equipment and preparing for adverse weather should really be looked at together. One essential item is a marine VHF radio. Most models include an area weather channel which smart captains tune to at the start of a trip and monitor from time to time during the day.

A marine radio is for your safety and convenience, but a Loran unit can both abet your safety and help you find fish. Loran, an acronym for Long Range Navigation, allows you to pinpoint your location by "tuning in" to three or more electronic pulses emitted by onshore towers. By knowing the Loran coordinates of a sunken wreck, for example, you can place your boat precisely over that wreck and enjoy whatever good fishing it might offer. However,

Loran can also allow for locational ranging well beyond visible land-marks, and can get you back to port in fog, snow, heavy rainfall or darkness. Once very expensive, Loran units are now within most any-one's budget, and such a unit is considered basic equipment on larger sport fishing vessels.

If a bad situation occurs, and you're anywhere far from shore, it's nice to know that someone back on land is aware of your general location and planned time of return. Tell someone where you're going and when you'll be back! It's the simplest yet one of the most important considerations for anyone boating big water.

Finally, instead of or in addition to your marine radio, have along a weather band radio—one that only tunes in to weather forecasts. In the Erie region, there are 24-hour harbor-by-harbor broadcasts that you can avail yourself of, to stay a step ahead of the big lake's quickly changing weather patterns.

Maps: Finding Top Bottoms

When scanning a map of the Great Lakes chain, Lake Erie appears to be a medium to small link in that chain. Contrasted with the irregular shorelines of Lake Superior or Huron, Erie looks like a small football rising or falling during a pass play.

Yet when boating a mile or two offshore, it becomes a wide expanse with few distinct shore markers and showing only gradual bottom contours on a sonar screen. Unlike the Canadian shield lakes to the north, Erie's bottom contours are not always easily readable. The use of Loran coordinates to establish "waypoints" (specific, pin-pointed locations which can be set and found later through electronic, navigational readings) makes location-finding much simpler. But successful fishing usually takes more than just Loran.

Compass points keyed to distinct shoreline features all help in location-finding when skies are clear and time allows for motoring around. Useful here are points, mountains, lighthouses, smokestacks, power plants and other large buildings.

Relatively inexpensive sonar units, available to fishermen for the past three decades, have served as a means to read depths and, if nothing else, indicate when the bottom is rising or falling so that the boater can at least get a general feel for what he's over. In all parts of Lake Erie except the islands area of the Western Basin, the bottom gradually rises as one approaches the U.S. shoreline. Even without a compass, a boater knows that shore lies somewhere in a southerly or southeasterly direction and can be reached by continually turning toward shallower depth readings.

But following the patterns of fish movements requires an overall understanding of the depths and changes in the lake's bottom. Hence, a good map will show bottom structures worth checking when yesterday's hot spot comes up cold today. Despite the relatively narrow band of waters along the U.S. shoreline of Lake Erie, open waters can be wide and frustrating.

Western Basin fishing areas appear to have more bottom structure than does the deeper Eastern Basin. In the west, sharp peninsulas and islands several miles offshore—some inhabited year-round—give the impression of being easily chartable for fishing. But any seasoned private or charter fisherman will confirm that finding fish sometimes results in 10- to 20-mile runs from shore over waters unmarked by points, islands or buoys.

Central and Eastern Basin areas offer even fewer visual markers for helping to find precise locations. No one wants to spend hours looking for likely alternatives or formerly good places that seem to change as fast as the sunlight, wind direction and wave heights. It's a big lake out there.

For these reasons, prior study of a good map can shorten search time and help improve the ratio of time on the water to fish-catching time. Quoting a serious-minded fisherman, "I come out here to catch fish—not to just go fishing." Serious and casual fishermen alike will do well to orient themselves with a good map before heading into "uncharted" waters.

Several map-making companies have developed maps of both large and small (specific) areas of Lake Erie. Here are some of them.

INLAND SPORTSMAN. These maps highlight the shoreline structures of the lake in a series of color patterns, clearly indicating dropoffs and likely fish-holding areas of Lake Erie's New York shoreline. Each map includes not only areas and place names, but also indicates dominant fish species, fishing techniques and tackle items, plus a seasonal rundown of approaches.

Inland Sportsman maps additionally provide navigational coordinates matching the popular Loran chains (Great Lakes or Northeastern U.S.) to visually check out locations in relation to shoreline configurations. Having both the readouts from an accurate Loran unit plus a good fishing-focused map can make open-water fish hunting an easier task.

NATIONAL OCEANIC SERVICE (NOS). These maps cover all areas of Lake Erie from Toledo to Buffalo. They're as large as 32 inches x 40 inches and are available in either folding paper or laminated plastic. The NOS maps replace the maps formerly available from Corp of Engineers offices in most populated centers along the Lake Erie shoreline.

DELORME MAPPING COMPANY. This company offers an "Atlas and Gazetteer" for each state bordering Erie (New York, Pennsylvania, Ohio and Michigan). Each map in the atlas includes general area information such as amusements, parks/forests, scenic drives, fishing sites, beaches, campgrounds, etc. These maps cover the shoreline; no bottom contours or other features are shown.

ERIE'S TRIANGLE. This company has produced a two-sided, laminated map of the Western Basin of Lake Erie, showing key navigational directions around the many islands in those waters and the locations of 42 recommended reefs situated in Canadian and U.S. waters between Point Pelee in Ontario, Vermilion in Ohio and Brest Bay in Michigan.

Before we move on to launching sites, a word should be said about "hook ups" for the private boater—organizations you can join to learn more about fishing Erie's waters, and in fact more about fishing in general.

Clubs are forming all along the Erie shoreline. From a practical standpoint, you might be best off simply finding the one that's closest to you. "Club" is a bit of a misnomer here since some of these groups now boast membership rolls of up to a thousand. One claims to have 3,000. A number of these organizations put out first-rate newsletters that contain a wealth of local, hard-core data on fishing

Erie or its tributaries. Some of the groups are named elsewhere in the book.

Where To Launch

It's a primary consideration for all private boaters: where can I drop my boat in with a minimum of cost, hassle, maneuvering and parking problems? There are already a fair number of places to launch a trailered boat along Erie's shoreline, and each year additional launches are added and improvements are made to existing ones.

Many new state-sponsored launch facilities have been built, and many existing ones have been expanded greatly to accommodate the increasing numbers of boaters. Ohio, for example, has a system of free launches, roughly 15 miles apart, each of which is protected by a breakwater or just natural geographic conditions. Michigan, with less than ten percent of the U.S. shoreline of Lake Erie, has in place two major sites (Bolles and Sterling State park) which can accommodate several hundred fishing boats each at one time. Also, two smaller launch facilities are open to the public so that a boat-trailering fisherman need travel less than 15 miles along the Michigan shoreline between Toledo and the Detroit River before arriving at another public access launch site.

Pennsylvania offers four area launch sites in the City of Erie and along the bay formed by Presque Isle. Additionally, Safe Harbor Marina at North East is scheduled for opening in 1991, and will offer 448 boating slips, storage for 120 boats and two free launch ramps.

New York's upgrading of Barcelona and Sturgeon Point facilities, plus its accesses at Dunkirk, Cattaraugus Creek and Buffalo provide five major access sites to the 90-mile shoreline of New York.

The following chart lists only the major areas, locales which offer two or more launch facilities. All these offer warm-weather launches. Check each location for specific season openings and closings, and daily hours of operation. Also inquire about the availability of fish-cleaning stations, expanded parking areas and extended periods of access (both daily and seasonal).

New York

BUFFALO. Small Boat Harbor, Erie Basin Marina, LaSalle Park and Ontario Street
EVANS. Sturgeon Point Marina (completely renovated in 1988)
CATTARAUGUS CREEK. Hanover Launch Ramp and two privately owned marinas
DUNKIRK. City-owned Pier and launch; one private launch
BARCELONA. Barcelona Harbor

Pennsylvania

NORTH EAST. Safe Harbor Marina (Set for completion Spring 1991)
ERIE. Three sites in this city
PRESQUE ISLE. Six sites in four locations

Ohio

CONNEAUT. Conneaut City Park
ASHTABULA. Three launches on the Ashtabula River
GENEVA. Geneva State Park
PAINESVILLE. Fairport Harbor and two on the Grand River
CLEVELAND. Six sites
LORAIN. Two sites
VERMILION. Two sites
HURON. Four sites
SANDUSKY BAY. Five sites
PORT CLINTON. Two sites
MARBLEHEAD. Dempsey and Mazurik access sites
TOLEDO. Five sites along the Maumee River Bay

Michigan

MONROE. Bolles Harbor and Sterling State Park.
Additional access sites exist in many locations which face open water and/or are too small for larger craft.

Places To Go and Fish

A large part of this book is intended to tell you where to go fish on Lake Erie. What follows here is just a brief summary of some of the more noteworthy destinations. Specific where-to information is scattered throughout many other chapters of the book.

BUFFALO. Walleye, smallmouth bass, and yellow perch along shoals outside of Buffalo Harbor. Buffalo also offers an extensive muskellunge fishery at the head of and into the passable waters of the upper Niagara River.

STURGEON POINT. Crowded with boaters during the spring and fall—not so much walleye fishermen as boaters looking to anchor and still fish for perch. Sturgeon also features miles of shallow bars. The Angola Bar (west of the point) provided Joe Thomas of Cincinnati the bulk of his bass poundage when he won first place in a recent bass tournament here.

CATTARAUGUS CREEK. Heavily stocked with salmonids, the creek provides eight to nine months of trout and salmon activity either in the creek or in lake waters just off its mouth. Near-shore and deep-water walleye fishing often occur at the same time of the season. Yellow perch school along many of the drop-offs, especially east of the creek.

DUNKIRK. Largest safe-water port west of Buffalo in New York State and surrounded with good shoreline and deep-water suspended walleye activity. Flat lining in early spring and anchoring for perch in the fall are top bets, but it's the walleye fishery that often lines vehicles and boat trailers along the side streets during weekdays in the summer. In winter, a power plant's warm water outflow draws small-boat anglers to cast, troll or still fish for salmon and trout.

BARCELONA. New York's deep-water port. Waters within 10 miles of Barcelona exceed 200 feet in depth and sometimes produce king salmon weighing more than 20 pounds. The mainstay for the harbor is a migrating population of suspended walleye which usually appear in area waters sometime in early June.

NORTH EAST. North East lies directly shoreward of the deep-

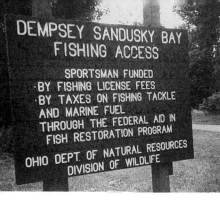

Public access sites and boat launches are numerous around the shores of Lake Erie, and the access situation will improve even further in the years ahead. When no public lauches are available in the immediate area, boaters can often find private facilities where they can put in for modest fees.

est waters of Lake Erie and has long reefs and other underwater structures infrequently fished. Smallmouth bass and yellow perch abound in these waters.

ERIE. Has the greatest number of launch sites and highest human population of any shore point in Pennsylvania. Erie anglers consistently take walleye and stocked salmonids in good sizes and numbers. A gill-netting fishery still exists in Pennsylvania, though it is closely monitored by the Pennsylvania Fish Commission. At this time, fewer than 15 commercial licenses are in effect.

CONNEAUT/ASHTABULA. Thousands of anglers fish from both ports and, notwithstanding movements of bait schools and the pursuing walleye, they essentially fish the same water. Conneaut has a well-protected city launch site and extensive charter boat complex. Ashtabula can boast several launches and well-equipped marinas along the Ashtabula River. Add the many nearby tributary fishing sites and the only difficulty is the decision as to where to fish first.

GENEVA STATE PARK. The Geneva launch site provides plenty of room to launch and good waters in which to fish. Approaches and tie-down areas well away from the launch ramps make this a model of the larger fishing access facilities. With good perch fishing most days of the summer and schools of suspended walleye several miles offshore, a day at Geneva in the middle of the summer (described later in this book) can be time rewardingly spent.

PAINESVILLE/FAIRPORT. With civic competition slightly less than in Conneaut/Ashtabula, this area also goes about its dual business of industry and sport fishing. There are charters and privately owned craft in great numbers here. Despite the high human population, clean water and good bottom contours make for great lake fishing and equally great tributary fishing in several area rivers and streams. Prediction: In years to come, this "center section" of the Central Basin will become as well known for steelhead fishing in the tribs as it is now known for perch and walleye fishing in the lake.

CLEVELAND. From Wildwood Park in the east to Lakewood just outside the city limits to the west, Cleveland's share of the shoreline offers six docking areas at which to find charter boats. Shoreline fishing during those warming spring days just after ice-out brings city and suburban anglers to piers and breakwaters. Party boats find perch and walleye near and far off Cleveland's shoreline, and trollers get a six to eight week share in the west-to-east migration of walleye each summer. Even when the fishing is off in the Cleveland area, it's usually only a short run east or west to make contact with active schools of fish.

LORAIN. Lorain has done everything but grow its own walleyes for the touring fisherman. The clean, bright Marina International is a docking complex of unmatched excellence. Hundreds of private, charter and party boats line the marina docking area and every type of Lake Erie fishing experience can be had from this one marina complex. For example, the largest head boat on Lake Erie, the 72-foot "Miss Majestic," is the first vessel seen as one begins walking the lengthy marina pier. In season, the rocky shoals and deeper dropoffs outside Lorain Harbor can offer perch, smallmouths, walleye and a surprising number of trout working bait schools off the mouth of the Black River.

VERMILION/HURON. Offering similar types of fishing, these two ports opened many new docking facilities during the 1980's. Channel systems and efficient docking configuration have expanded the private and chartering boat presence in this area remarkably. Already known for its walleye and perch fishing, these ports are gaining increasing attention as bass fishing destinations.

SANDUSKY BAY. This area has it all. The islands lie just around Marblehead Point and the deeps lie just a few miles to the east. A well-powered boater can fish two basins with less than an hour's run from the mouth of Sandusky Bay. Add the web of natural streams that course their way into the inner bay area and Sandusky is good afloat or afoot. The Sandusky River and main feeders such as Muddy, Muskellunge and Wolf Creeks are augmented with large upstream feeders like Honey Creek, many of which reach south to distances greater than 25 miles. More than 100 miles of fishable tributary waters await the energetic stream fisherman willing to take the hike.

PORT CLINTON/CATAWBA ISLAND/MARBLEHEAD. Offers more charter boats per square mile than any other port system on Lake Erie. This area was, collectively, one of the first hotspots when Erie's sport fishing was rediscovered. Drifting headboaters have been upgrading techniques to deal with the gradually increasing water clarity they are finding here. The big fishing news in this area is the remarkable number of trollers seen in recent years around the islands of the Western Basin (more about this topic in later chapters).

TOLEDO/MONROE, MICHIGAN. Two distinct population areas each with several fishing centers. Toledo has eight docking areas along the shores of the Maumee Bay and River; Monroe has two major launch sites (Sterling State Park and Bolles Harbor). The latter also supports chartering. A few charter boats run down the Detroit River and work in U.S. waters. Although the Michigan waters of Lake Erie do not exceed 25 feet, the spring and early summer run of walleye here is legendary.

Chapter 5

A Lake for All Seasons

There is some fishing available, somewhere on Lake Erie or its tributaries, all year long. But that does not imply that your spot will bear fruit on the day you visit it. From year to year, there can be extensive fluctuation even at some of Erie's most time-proven hot spots. Further, within the same year, a hot location can go cold very quickly. Erie the "cat," as described in Chapter One, is an elusive and changeable body of water, one that mandates continual adjustment in one's trip planning and one's fishing strategies.

This chapter is intended to "set the table" for you, with a glimpse at Erie's opportunities as they progress from early season to late season. In Parts II and III, many of these specific types of fishing will be examined in greater detail.

Ice covers much of the lake during the dead of winter. Depending on the weather, this phenomenon will begin in November or December and end in February or March. Year-round, open-water boating access can be found at several major tributaries and harbors.

All Winter Tributaries

Major tributaries generally remain fishable all winter, but severe weather, periods of extremely high water, or ice blockage can shut down even the largest tribs.

It may require a hardy, spirited approach and well-insulated waders and clothing, but the rivers and streams that flow into Lake Erie provide a backdrop for many a fish-fighting experience all year long. Steelhead ascend many rivers and are the top winter-time challenge in the tributaries. Brown trout of hefty sizes are frequently chanced upon side by side with the silver battlers; browns ascend many tributaries when the fall spawning urge strikes (October-November) and they are also known to shadow other spawning salmonids so they can feast on whatever fish eggs become available.

Neither the coho nor the king salmon mount the spectacular runs which occur in Lake Ontario tributaries, but some stream action for fall salmon does occur. There is much more on all this in Part III.

A Perch and Salmonid Stew

Once the ice finally disappears from the surface and shoreline of the lake, active anglers are met with several alternatives and considerable decision-making.

Two fisheries dominate the ice-out period on Lake Erie: Shallow-water fishing for the assortment of trout and salmon that move close to shore immediately after surface ice disappears—even as ice mounds up and lingers along the shoreline; and deep-water yellow perch fishing for schooling, pre-spawn fish. Once ice disappears in early spring, many schools of perch hold in deep water (rather than move into near-shore shallows) often in the general area in which they were found by ice fishermen. But many also move in close where they are met by eager anglers.

Both salmonids and perch, activated by opening waters and an increase of oxygenated water, take up locations in relatively confined and targetable waters. This is not to say that there will necessarily be easy pickins, but the starting points are fewer and better defined than at other times.

Both shore anglers (either casting lures or working a live or natural bait rig) and boaters trolling the shallows can get in on the busy salmonid fishery that begins just after ice-out.

Bank and pier fishermen take a two-fisted approach to shore fishing. Because it's never known before an outing whether the fish will be actively hitting cast lures or sinker-held live or natural baits, many anglers work out a two-rod system. One rod, often referred to as the "dead rod," is set up with a live minnow, worm or grub, and a second rod is set up for casting fairly small, weighted spoons like Kastmasters, Krocodiles, KO Wobblers, Little Cleos, etc. Also used are spinners such as Mepps, Super Vibrax, Panther Martins, Rooster Tails and so on.

Where to fish is much easier to pinpoint than when to fish. Shortly after ice-out most piers will draw schools of perch both yellow and white, and white (silver) bass, but when ice-out will occur or when the fish schools will arrive are highly unpredictable. The best approach is simply to look for ice-out and keep your ears peeled for talk of fish moving inshore.

Folk wisdom offers advice on the perch run. One of the most celebrated bits of local lore has the perch run coinciding with the first bloom of lilacs. Regardless of the presence or absence of lilacs in the neighborhood, the best barometer of action is the number of anglers gathered along piers and docks. The early spring perch run may last as long as three or four weeks, but the frantic feeding activity usually only lasts a week or two.

Ice-out casting for salmonids is the other fast and furious action in early spring. While lake trout was the dominant native species of salmonid in Lake Erie waters in its storied past, steelhead and brown trout took well when stocked in tributaries and embayments in the Eastern Basin. These are top early season targets. Add the coho and occasional chinook salmon to the mix, and the spring shoreline at times is buzzing and bustling.

When the run is on, tributary and harbor fishermen can be seen at every hour of the day. But peak of activity occurs at first light. Devoted shore anglers, afoot or in small craft, get out well before sunlight and set up rods with live bait rigs, as well as with artificial lures.

Lure and location changes become necessary when there are no clear signs of fish activity. Spring runs of trout present anglers with constantly changing conditions. The morning when a quick limit came on egg sacks in shallow, calm waters may be followed by a morning when only deeper waters in the current or the tail of a pool produce pickups and strikes.

As in all fishing situations where conditions change constantly, go with the motto: when in doubt, move about. Pet lures, honey-hole hotspots and the best casting techniques known will all fail if the fish have switched their movements and feeding patterns from the day or week before. Experience with spring-run salmonids teaches us to check stream and nearshore water conditions, to keep in mind the variety of natural and artificial baits possible for catching these fish, and to not presume that every spring the fish will move into the shoreline and feed in shallow water in the same manner. Variety is the spice of spring salmonid life.

This walleye could qualify as trophy size on most any walleye lake, but on Erie, a five to eight-pounder is far from a wall fish. Most anglers wait until a ten pounder comes along before visiting the local taxidermist.

Walleye: Openers and Openings

Some years will begin with considerable chatter about walleye fishing around Port Clinton as soon as Cleveland's I-X Center opens for the Sport, Travel & Outdoor Show in early March. These reports come from individual anglers and early-running charter boat fishermen who have been out and around the islands, checking out the popular shore, shoal and reef areas where walleye will begin staging before the annual spawning ritual. In other years, late ice and unfavorable winds put sport fishing forecasts on hold until sometime around the perch and walleye spawning season, which is primarily April.

State-regulated walleye season openers vary from state to state. At this writing, New York and Pennsylvania impose a closed walleye season from March 15 until the first Saturday in May. Ohio, however, does not close walleye season during the spawning period.

Bass: A Fish for All Comers

Bass season opener on Lake Erie draws increasing attention each new season, even though the fervor that ensues in no way matches the one that builds towards the opening of walleye season. "Underutilized" is a word which sees frequent use in discussions and written material on the subject of smallmouth bass fishing here.

Bass season in New York opens the third Saturday in June and extends to November 30th. Lake Erie is not excepted from this. Bass can be caught here throughout this time period but the best time is probably late June until mid-July—when the water approaches the 70 degree mark.

Musky Mania

While muskellunge populations are not high in Lake Erie, the few spots where they do gather make for much talk and action. Two areas in the Eastern Basin maintain holding populations of muskies: Presque Isle Bay and the Niagara River. These two areas offer completely different fishing situations. Presque Isle Bay is a large, shallow-water area where fish relate to weed beds and channel edges. The fishing is similar to conditions on Chautauqua Lake. As the water temperatures rise and weed growth develops, muskies move either deep into the weeds or well away from the edges that are so popular in the spring and fall seasons. This early-summer movement may account for the muskies that are caught 20 and 30 miles away from conventional musky cover along Lake Erie's shoreline. The musky mecca of Lake Erie and in fact the whole region has to be the upper stretches of the Niagara River. Fishery biologists have been looking at the possibility that these river fish are a subspecies of muskellunge, although no key has been written to firmly establish a distinction. Despite the lack of a scientific statement, Niagara River muskies certainly have distinct behavioral patterns.

These fish spend their entire lives in currents of varying speeds. They are nomadic and are often caught well out into the lake in what is called "the head of the river." A large musky will feed on five-pound or larger walleye, other assorted gamefish and smaller muskies.

The late Clarence Gall of North Tonawanda trolled large, tuned plugs over the weed and rock shoals around Strawberry and Grand Islands with the accuracy of an experienced target shooter. Gall's lures ran to all depths in current and his skill at boat handling is something only time and repeated observation can develop.

It is well understood among "musky men" that this is not a sport for those who like to catch a lot of fish. A banner day is one in which three fish are hooked and one or two fish are caught. At two selected times of the year, early summer and early fall weed die-off, good numbers of fish can be caught, but these fish rarely reach trophy size. The true trophies are usually conquered during late fall.

Lake Erie and upper Niagara River regulations allow possession of muskies at a minimum length of 30 inches; the lower Niagara regulation has been set at a 44-inch minimum. Since prime breeding fish range in length from the high 20's to about 40 inches, musky-minded sporting organizations suggest that anglers consider taking only true trophy-size fish; and use a gentle hand on the smaller fish when releasing them.

When Summer Turns to Fall

Fall is a season of distinct change on Lake Erie. Steelhead start to run into feeder streams and major tributaries, perch school along structures closer to shore and walleye enter into their final warm-weather feeding stages. Every fall season begins and develops differently, but the major shifts occur with the shortening of daylight hours in mid-September. Another natural sign is the first frost, which may occur anytime between early September and early October.

Boat and shoreline traffic subsides, as many fishermen turn to the hunting of small and big game. Foliage changes seen on land are also evident in the aquatic foliage, signalling a change in water conditions.

Fall steelhead and perch fishing is covered in greater detail elsewhere in this book. One iffy fall fishing prospect is the catching of walleye when they are supposed to be "feeding up" for the winter. The concept should be looked at with some skepticism. True, Lake Erie anglers sometimes come in from a fall outing with a limit of big walleye in a short period of time. They also take long boat rides and go fishless, even as they pass anchored boaters who might well be filling buckets with perch nearing the one-pound mark.

The realization that walleye sometimes feed at suspended depths at midday, even at times in bright sunlight and near-tropical heat, has forced serious walleye fishermen to revise their thinking about the nocturnal, bottom-hugging image this fish has had. It stands to reason that if metabolic rates rise and fall with the changes in water temperature, bait fish and walleye should "feed up" when their activity level and forage is highest.

Yet catch results at certain times (never predictable) indicate big walleye can be taken at both suspended levels with downriggers and planer boards, and along bottom structures with spinner and worm or three-way rigs and lures. The key phrase here is "at times." Walleye schooling patterns in fall are very dicey, and are influenced by water temperatures, bait school movements, dominant wind patterns and just plain moods. The best approach is just to give it a try, but take along some gear for yellow perch—just in case. The walleye-only fall fishing trip may result in much more fishing than catching.

Ice: The Ins and Outs

It sometimes happens that, during long periods of sub-zero temperatures with low winds, Lake Erie's entire surface will be covered with ice. More typically, safe ice only forms at the extreme eastern and western ends of the lake, as well as in many enclosed bays and harbors. Thus, more than 90 percent of the nearly ten thousand square miles of Lake Erie's surface is usually unsafe for ice fishing.

Most harbors form safe ice which can provide some great panfishing experiences for thousands dressed for the cold. One notable exception is the ice formed at Dunkirk Harbor. The warm-water outflow from the power plant at the west end of the harbor holds the water temperature above freezing all winter long. On most days, small boats can be launched from the city pier.

Buffalo Harbor and many large bays around Grand Island support large numbers of ice anglers mostly in search of smelt and perch. But, when weather conditions allow, the open water of Lake Erie between Buffalo and the Town of Evans can result in perch catches which match size with those taken from New York's famed inland lakes. Also, walleye and the occasional lake trout make ice fishing in the Eastern Basin well worth enduring the cold.

When Lake Erie ice fishing finally gets under way, piles of perch can surround every well-chosen hole in the ice. Sad to relate, those same areas that were so hot a week or year previous may be dangerous or inaccessible this week or year. See Chapter 16 for important data on safe ice fishing.

Western Basin perch and walleye ice fishing has not only come of age, it's gone commercial. The prime consideration here is to call ahead. While the fishing can be terrific and a booming hut industry has emerged around the islands north of Port Clinton and Catawba Island, weather and ice conditions change rapidly in the relatively flat lands surrounding the northwestern Ohio-southeastern Michigan shoreline of Lake Erie. Local hut operators, bait and tackle stores and area chambers of commerce will give advice as to fishing possibilities. So much depends on the weather that this area, like the open water west of Buffalo, calls for a regular check on ice formation and current weather conditions. Some years have afforded weeks and even a couple of months of safe ice fishing. Other years do not offer safe ice conditions all winter long. At times, the ice forms and is gone before the local experts can get out, make contact with good fish and come back with favorable reports.

Part Two

50 Years
A Lake Erie Fisherman

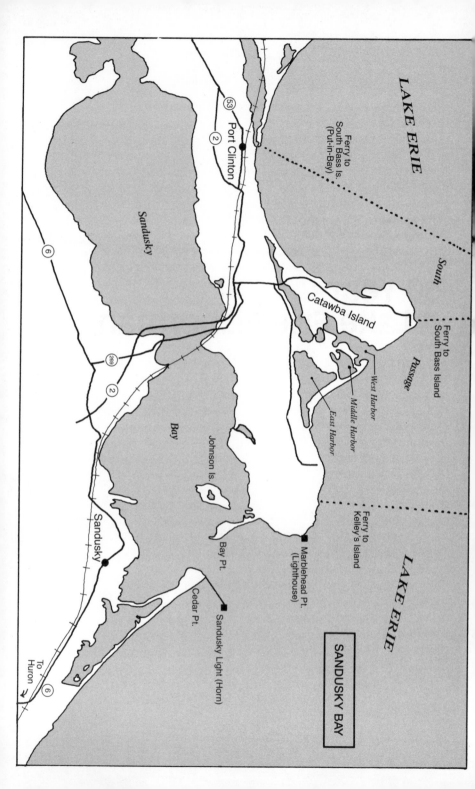

LAKE ERIE

⑤③
Port Clinton
②

Sandusky

⑥

②⑬
②

Ferry to
South Bass Is.
(Put-in-Bay)

South

Catawba Island

Passage

Ferry to
South Bass Island

West Harbor

Middle Harbor

East Harbor

Bay

Johnson Is.

Sandusky

Ferry to
Kelley's Island

Bay Pt.

Marblehead Pt.
(Lighthouse)

LAKE ERIE

Cedar Pt.

Sandusky Light (Horn)

To
Huron

⑥

SANDUSKY BAY

Chapter 6

Ice Out Opportunities

Whil e the ranks of year-round anglers grows steadily, with steelheaders and ice fishermen the main contributors to that growth, the greater number of fishermen on Lake Erie still wait till the ice disappears and the air temperature at least tries to hold above the freezing point.

The majority of cabin-cribbed fishermen have their first opportunity to make at least vicarious contact with the sport of fishing by attending a late-winter, early-spring fishing exposition. Next to the passing of ice, the surest sign of spring is the arrival of these fishing shows in towns and cities along the Erie shoreline.

These worthwhile expos offer technique-oriented seminars on many aspects of fishing in nearby waters. Annually, a schedule of speakers is drawn from the ranks of TV fishing personalities, regional guides and charter captains, well-known outdoor writers and state and local fisheries experts. The shows also offer exhibits of new and interesting tackle items of potential use in the area of that show. Everything from new lines of hooks or lures to offshore dream boats crowd their way into auditoriums, convention centers and arenas from Toledo to Buffalo.

Charter captains and resort operators invariably take up several aisles. These people can put you onto fishing locations and approaches with just a few brochures and several minutes worth of conversation. This is apt to be insider's information that might take weeks or months for you to gather on your own.

The biggest annual fishing exhibit related to Lake Erie is the American & Canadian Sport, Travel & Outdoor Show held each year in mid-March at the I-X Center in Cleveland, Ohio. This 10-day event, presented each spring for more than 50 years, features 3,000-plus exhibitors inside an open 16-acre complex. Representatives from four states and Canada provide fishermen with regional information, including info relating to Lake Erie. It will take more than a day to see just the fishing-related exhibits and events at this show.

Buffalo's Great Lakes Fishing & Outdoor Exposition is another major draw for feverish anglers in search of data and direction on the expanded fisheries in Lake Erie's Eastern Basin. Scheduled a week or two after the Cleveland show, Buffalo's "Expo" is a prime source of information for anglers at all levels of sophistication—bobbers to downriggers.

Then there are the shows offered along the Erie shoreline at Erie, Conneaut, Ashtabula, Sandusky, and Toledo; plus the shows in not too distant Rochester, NY, Harrisburg, PA and Detroit, MI, all with Lake Erie-related exhibits. All in all, several days in early spring can be pleasantly spent on the expo trail.

The Shoreline's Fine

Even many shoreline residents here miss out on one of the most fruitful aspects of fishing Lake Erie: shore casting immediately after ice-out. Admittedly, the cold, clear water of the lake at first seems less than promising. With water temperatures slightly above freezing, fish movements may indeed be minimal. When action begins, though, it can begin decisively. When brown and rainbow trout plus coho and king salmon begin their spring run toward the tributaries, shorelines can be highly productive. Water temperature becomes a key factor in finding these shorebound fish, and tributary outlets often provide just the right combination: warmer temperatures, well oxygenated water and concentrations of baitfish.

Boaters search both deep and shallow. When game fish do move close to shore, it's often on a hit-and-move basis. Casting small but heavy spoons and spinners around tributary mouths can be productive. Skillful positioning of the boat is often one of the secrets of success.

Current flow becomes easier to ascertain when the stream water is stained or muddied and distinct in coloration from that of the lake. These "mud lines" serve as ambush points for gamefish to strike at disoriented bait fish that move into and out of this darker water. Casters position their boats along either side of such a mud line and work spoons or spinners in and out of this water. The more successful direction of casting depends on how the fish are hitting at the moment. Wind direction, sunlight penetration and movements of bait schools all dictate where to put the lure, but these factors may change in minutes as the angler is working a given stretch of water.

Casters working from shore at times have a distinct advantage over the more mobile boaters, because stream-headed salmonids often run in waters shallower than boaters can navigate. Breakwaters provide good platforms for those not wishing to wade frigid waters. First light is often prime time. Cold, calm mornings—often beginning in a shroud of ground fog—create a quiet but exciting backdrop for this type of trout and salmon fishing.

It's true enough that shoreline access in places is difficult, and that wading in near-freezing water is rigorous. Further, finding the fish can take a while. But the search can be shortened by working shorelines adjacent to tributary mouths and prominent points along the shoreline. These are the top spots. Most major tributaries have private or state-owned access sites where pier fishermen or wading anglers may start out in search of salmonids along shore.

Lures hang by the hundreds in local bait and tackle shops. Several popular casting spoons get mentioned every season: Little Cleos, Kastmasters, KO Wobblers and Sidewinders are among them. Look for two to four-inch spoons in the 1/4- to 3/4-ounce sizes. Spinners also draw considerable attention: Super Vibrax, Mepps, Rooster Tails and Panther Martins are among the very popular ones. Some anglers even buy the components from fishing supply catalogs and fashion their own lures.

When casting spinners, choose a body and blade configuration that will work effectively in the currents and openings being plied. A slow but pulsating movement in these situations is essential. Tie in a small but efficient swivel to minimize line twisting and subsequent development of weak spots in the line. It's worth the slightly higher cost to purchase high quality ball bearing swivels. Twisted line is not only a nuisance but will eventually lead to loss of a good fish when weak points develop in the line.

Line weight varies, but most casters go relatively light with four to eight pound test. The lighter lines cast better and most of these early season salmonids weigh less than ten pounds. Also, the lighter lines tend to be less visible to the fish in the clear water of early spring.

In states that allow fishing with two lines, many shorecasters looking for trout and salmon also set up a "dead" rod while casting spoons and spinners. Often the dead rod is anything but. When set

up properly, it frequently takes more fish than the one sending out lures. Typically, the second rod is set up with some kind of live or fresh-dead bait. The number one live bait in the cold waters of spring has to be the minnow. Worms and nightcrawlers will catch salmonids at times, but minnow-dunking gets the best results. This is not to say that the minnow is simply hooked on and thrown out. Serious shore anglers put as much thought and preparation into the second line as is given to the line set up for casting.

Two important concerns are minnow size and hooking techniques. At times, smaller minnows of the size you'd use for perch will work better—even with the larger trout and salmon. This will be most true when the fish are feeding on schools of smaller bait fish.

How the minnow is hooked depends on certain factors. If the line is set in a fixed position and there is little current, a fine wire hook through the back (behind the dorsal fin) will allow the bait to move around and look appealing. A lip-hooked minnow offers more appeal when worked in either moving current or when the bait is being repeatedly cast and retrieved.

Egg sacks and skein, fresh or prepared, run a close second. Size can matter. Generally, when waters are clear, smaller sacks or bait sections on light lines are necessary. With some stain or turbidity to the water, larger sacks or skein sections can be used.

Most states require that fishing lines be attended at all times. But even a smaller (one or two pound) brown or coho can hit a minnow and begin moving along the shoreline at rod-ripping speeds. Attention to the second rod used in salmonid waters is a must. Check that the drag setting is such that it barely holds line on the spool; strikes can then often be detected by the sound of the yielding drag as it starts to click.

Usually, a forked stick or just a rock for propping up the rod will make do at most shore sites. However, serious shore anglers use either clamp-on rod holders or run a small bungie cord around the rod handle above the reel. Even if the drag releases properly and line loops do not get in the way, you still may have to quickly jump for your rod. Sudden strikes from early season trout and salmon have sent more than one rod and reel combination flying into the drink.

Perching Offshore

At the same time that shore anglers are hitting into various-sized schools of perch along the shallows around docks, piers and points, big schools of pre and post spawn perch gather well offshore on or near the bottom at depths of 30 to 50 feet or more. This dichotomy leaves many experts groping for an explanation. While they're groping, we can enjoy the fishing.

Despite the availability of minnow forage, stomach contents indicate that when perch are feeding in early spring the main forage is bottom life: grubs, snails, water worms etc. Minnows only make up a small part of their diet. Still, the top bait for these deep water perch is the minnow. Grubs, worms, nightcrawlers and perch eyes all take a few perch when the fish are hitting steadily. But for consistent action under most conditions, minnows are best.

Wind direction has a direct influence, even in deep water of 30 to 50 feet where wave action would not appear to have any effect. Winds from the south or west usually signal good deep-water perch fishing. Have a wind shift to northerly or easterly and bad things begin to happen in even the deepest waters of Lake Erie. The fish either become more difficult to find and catch or they simply stop hitting altogether. Good graph recorders may confirm heavy perch schools holding tight to the bottom during these off periods; the fish can easily see the variously colored and baited rigs sent down and held within striking distance of these perch. The fish just turn off for a while and either peck at the baits or become completely inactive.

There can be dramatic changes even from one day to the next. After a great day with buckets overflowing, the day following may be accompanied by a wind shift to north or east and the fishing goes sour. Even within the same day, a wind change can turn the fishing on—or off. Then anglers may be forced to reposition over alternate structures, or even pull anchor and quit for the day.

When things get tough during adverse wind conditions, the trip can be saved with some creative sonar probing and anchor placement. When conditions are right, perch can be found on a sonar dial or graph readout as they hold just above the bottom along vast stretches of rock or gravel. But, as winds change or cold fronts move through, the fish seem to move off the screen and leave the easily targetable open flats along the bottom.

Even when fish go off feed they still can sometimes be enticed into striking. Attractors become important. For example, you can try variously colored beads, small spinners and in-line propellers. Small spinner blades—sometimes called "flickers"—with either yellow, chartreuse, fluorescent orange or red, silver or gold finishes perk up inactive fish quickly. When fixed to both ends of the newer styles of fine-wire spreaders, these brightly colored flickers may mean the difference between catching fish and just fishing.

Colors can become just as critical as when selecting crankbaits for bass or suspended walleye. The metallic finishes (silver and gold) seem to work in either sunny or cloudy weather, with gold a better choice when skies are overcast. Greens and yellows both have their moments, but yellow is generally better on sunny days in clear water. The reds and oranges can work all day, but they seem to get more attention toward evening.

Structure, too, becomes more important when the perch turn off. When schools are clearly visible on sonar they are usually either heavily feeding on bait fish or grubbing along the bottom. But when they go off-feed, they relate more closely to structural changes in the bottom. Most often, this means drop-offs.

Why perch hold along drop-offs is a matter of speculation. They may be seeking cover with favorable escape routes from predators or they may be using the bottom contours to ambush bait without having to travel too far from bottom. Whatever the reason, the result is that fishermen can find them here.

On structure, the catches generally will be less than those taken on halcyon days when the fish hit as soon as the bait gets near bottom and (where two lines are allowed) the angler cannot even work two rods. But a bad trip can be saved and a few good fish can be put in the bucket with some patience and careful attention to details.

Panfish Inshore
Panfishing can be adult-level fun, and indeed it is on Lake Erie. With wide expanses of hard rock shoals and shallow drop-offs along the entire

shoreline of the lake, panfish are abundant. As mentioned earlier, yellow perch move close to shore in spring to both spawn and seek out additional forage as their metabolism speeds up in the increasingly warm waters. These shallows are also visited by two non-native species which were introduced to Lake Erie waters some decades ago and have steadily increased in numbers: white perch and white bass.

White perch (*Morone americana*) are not really white and do not belong to the perch family. In fact, a white perch is silver/gray/olive with lateral striping similar to that of a striped bass (*Morone saxatilis*). The fish is classified not as a perch but a bass. White bass (often called "silver bass") are, indeed, silver in coloration and do belong to the bass family.

Both white bass and white perch became more abundant with the decline of the blue pike in Lake Erie. But many anglers seeking larger gamefish, for example walleye and black bass, consider white bass and white perch nuisance fish. Their sharp, spiny fins cause many minor cuts to the hands of anglers who are careless in removing hooks from these fish. They are small, usually less than 10 inches, and less than desirable when caught in small numbers. They generally move in large, often suspended schools and tend to force the larger fish (bass and walleye) out of the area. When encountering these suspended panfish, most serious walleye trollers retrieve their planer boards or downriggers and move to another spot.

As for food value, the popular notion is that these fish are less desirable than yellow perch or the smaller walleyes. I disagree. The problem may be that they're just not cared for as well as they should be. When either of these fish is kept on a stringer or in a water-filled cooler for a prolonged period of time, the meat deteriorates more rapidly than the flesh of most other fish species. In particular, try cleaning and cooking these fish as soon as possible after they are caught.

Another Lake Erie panfish is the dependable rock bass. Lake Erie's shoreline structure allows rockies to grow to good sizes and most of them feel little pressure from sport fishermen. Unlike yellow perch, white bass and white perch, bragging-sized rock bass usually do not school and cannot be caught in great numbers while the boat is anchored in one fixed place.

Either a slow drift or a continual repositioning with an electric trolling motor will allow the presentation of a worm-tipped jig, a top lure for these structure-holding fish. Most anglers hook into these big rockies while bottom-bumping for smallmouths. Many anglers begin to realize that these fish, pound for pound, offer the same sport as black bass; and of course anglers can keep rock bass in any size and number.

The first stirrings of rock bass usually occur after most other panfish have already become active. They don't usually hit in good numbers until the water temperature approaches 50 degrees. The presence of rock bass, for most summer fishermen, signals the start of early-summer fishing activities.

One final note on rockies: there is no better time to show a kid or rookie angler how to effectively fish a jig than early-summer fishing for rock bass. While on a slow drift over rock bottom, a beginner can get a feel for working a jig at various speeds without getting tangled up with the business of casting and retrieving.

Jigs, a real workhorse lure around these parts, take more than their share of Lake Erie fish. Becoming proficient with them will help you to take many of the other Erie targets discussed at length in the following chapters.

Chapter 7

Springing Forth

Western and Central Basin ports bustle with party and head boat activity as water temperatures begin their rapid rise. Schooling fish, especially walleye, gather in definable patterns which make party boat fishing productive and fun.

Ice-out around the Western Basin islands in recent seasons has seen more and more anglers out in small and large boats. They may now even outnumber the casters who traditionally gather along the banks of the spawning streams and rivers northeast of Toledo.

For the angler unfamiliar with the famed Western Basin of Lake Erie, an outing or two on any of the popular party boats might be a better approach than a series of solo tries to discover where and how to fish in the early spring. Head boats begin working out of Toledo, Port Clinton, Sandusky, Huron and many other ports as soon as ice disappears and word of that gets around.

Tackle should include a smooth-casting, light to medium rod and reel combination. For years, experienced anglers told newcomers to stick with spinning reels. However, the newest generation of small, light, level-wind reels cast with ease and efficiency. The new reels have high retrieval ratios (4:1 or more) to avoid the excessive hand-cranking chore that low-retrieval reels used to force on fishermen. Prices still remain higher than comparable spinning reels, but competition among major tackle manufacturers is steadily lowering the price.

One good reason for being able to cast a little farther these days is the increasing water clarity in the shallows of the Western Basin as well as all other areas of Lake Erie. Clear water is nice to look at, but it allows fish to detect the approach of a boat and recognize artificial lures more quickly. Charter captains now start drifts well above the moving schools of suspended walleye and do not start engines or make unnecessary noises until ready to pull up and head for another location.

Perhaps the best adaptation to this clearer water is lighter line. The finer lines tend to spook fish less as those fish move in to check out your spinner and worm, or whatever. It is not impossible to run six-pound or even four-pound test line when the water looks gin clear and the winds are barely moving the boat. One Erie regular remarked to me that he uses only four-pound line unless the water "gets dirty and there's a heavy chop." In fact, in springtime a "heavy chop" may actually amount to heavy seas, but even with these conditions, the use of lighter lines may increase the catch or shorten the time needed to put together a legal limit.

All party boats are equipped to land a heavy walleye. No one need lift a fish from the water in order to get it into the boat. In light of this, and the increasingly clear water, using a lighter line just might improve your spring and summer walleye catches.

For boat-trailering fishermen who haven't been to the Western Basin in the early spring in recent years, some positive changes have taken place. The entirely new Mazurik Launch Site on the lake side of Marblehead opened in 1989 and the Dempsey-Sandusky Bay site has been upgraded and vastly improved.

All-Points Perch

While early spring walleye fishing draws many to areas where the season is open just after the ice melts, the universal object of most early-season Lake Erie anglers is the plentiful schools of yellow perch. They begin schooling just before the ice begins to disappear in that thermal inversion which occurs early each spring as the water temperature begins to approach 39 degrees.

Ice sinks during this thermal inversion, but in calm water it usually melts before reaching depths of 20 feet. Yellow perch begin staging below this winter-to-spring turnover, and now the fun begins.

An early arrival of spring-like weather does not assure good perch fishing as much as does a gradual and consistent rise in water temperatures coupled with a minimum of easterly winds. Prevailing winds on Lake Erie vary from the Eastern to the Western Basin. In general, prevailing winds in the Eastern Basin are from the southwest, with westerly winds holding during long periods of a somewhat steady wind direction. In the Central and Western Basin, however, westerly winds prevail. Somewhere between Barcelona and Erie a subtle shift in dominant wind direction occurs. It may be merely a coincidence, but that wind shift occurs at about the same location as Lake Erie's greatest depths (about 210 feet).

Along with consistent temperature increases and prevailing winds, look for normal rainfall and normal stream runoff. Some perch hunters look for stained water, some run out to clear water and some begin the search for perch along any visible mudline set up between muddied and clear water.

Curiously, good catches of perch can come from all three of these locations. While the suspended mud particles tend to heat ambient waters, the more clear waters afford the fish an opportunity to seek out the more visible bait schools.

One of the first considerations is to determine the forage on which the perch are feeding. The first fish brought into the boat should be checked out thoroughly. If possible, look at disgorged particles as the fish is being reeled in. Look down its throat to see what food remnants may be inside its mouth. Much can be learned from what the fish are eating. The presence of minnows in the gullet suggests the perch are on the move and may be either traveling back and forth along a food shelf, or they may be moving from the area. The presence of bug life (scud, freshwater shrimp, water worms and other bottom-holding creatures) indicate the fish are scrubbing along the bottom and may be holding tight to that bottom in a generally fixed location. Another sign to look for is possible scraping and chafing on the tip of the lower jaw, indicating that the fish has been foraging in stone and gravel bottoms.

Anchoring may seem like a simple task. Find a likely spot to stop and fish, throw the anchor over the side and start fishing. When luck prevails, fish start hitting and cleaning time is longer than catching time. But anyone who has been sitting at a distance and watching nearby boaters pull in fish after fish knows that boat placement can be critical.

Veteran perch fishermen swear that perch follow even the slightest of channels and move along edges of drop-offs in patterns as regular as trout in small streams. Party and charter boat captains keep elaborate records of these seasonal movements and depths. Expert recreational fishermen, too, follow the perch school's pre- and post-spawn movements.

Generally, the spring movement of perch is from deeper to shallower waters; the fall movement is from mid-depths to deep waters just before the formation of ice in early winter. But all good perch fishermen take steps each spring to find a deep-water starting point. That is, with the efficient use of sonar equipment, boaters move out steadily, checking each structural change (drop-off, sunken island, channel, etc.) for possible schooling perch. Most often, the fish are located at depths a few feet either side of a magic number.

In deeper areas of the lake, perch seem to school at approximately 55 feet of water during both the spring and fall change-of-season periods—before and after the formation of ice. While early-summer anglers happily hit into schools of perch at mid-depths in many locations, the key to early-spring perching generally involves a run out to 55 feet or deeper. That's where you're apt to find the largest schools of perch.

Once good perch schools are found, the task is simplified but not complete. Sudden temperature changes, high winds, rainfall and other types of weather can all contribute to the fish going off feed.

Hundreds of boating anglers set anchors and fish for perch each

The railings along Cleveland's docks and piers support many a fishing rod when the perch begin moving close to shore each spring.

spring, often very close together. A mysterious magnetism draws boaters together when the lake is so large, the fish are so deep and the fisherman is so acutely aware that his own boat is just a speck on a giant inland sea. Rather than carefully watch weather, water and other conditions, most boaters leave the harbor and simply look for heavy concentrations of anchored boats on the presumption that these boaters have already found the fish.

Whether they have or not, it's a starting point on a lake with few visible markers. While many complain about the crowding that can ensue, the smart perch hunter moves through these flotillas and does his own planning. At times the gang gets into the fish; at times, they simply keep each other company. It takes a little experience to get the right read on a group of boaters you encounter.

Use these "boat herds" as a control in searching out perch, but don't lose sight of what your own boat is doing. Knowing how deep you are, and what's on the bottom, will be essential in the continuous effort to determine where to stop and when to go. All fishing situations call for some serious decision-making from time to time, but perch fishing in the open, unmarked waters of Lake Erie seems to force the moment to its crisis. Sometimes an anchoring point will only turn up schools of juvenile perch. Sometimes anchoring within even feet of a boat that's scoring will not pan out. Exactly when to move can be a tough call.

If your party is out mainly for fun and fresh air, constant anchor-pulling may well damper that fun. When a serious catch of perch is the aim, frequent moves may be necessary. Without fully disregarding the moves and site selections of other boaters, the better approach is to find good bottom structures, which show sonar readings of both bait and perch schools. Then, send out a combination of rigs that have been effective in past outings, plus rigs that speak to any new theories you might have come up with.

Throwing Shoreline Curves

Fishing for perch in shallow waters during the spring is as overlooked as the smallmouth bass fishing in Lake Erie. Those boaters just mentioned—the ones drawn to deep water by other boaters—may be missing a shallow-water event which occurs along many rock and gravel shorelines along Lake Erie. It's the "evening run" of perch.

Boaters need only a good pair of oars to reach many of these evening-feeding perch schools, as they move into depths of less than 10 feet. Perch will sometimes chase minnows in a pre-spawn feeding foray closely matching the feeding of pre-spawn walleye.

When the water temperature rises and begins to approach 40 degrees, about the time the shoreline run of trout and salmon begins to taper, perch move in and out of shallow water...and there are few fishing boats there to greet them. Depending mostly on when ice-out occurs, this phenomenon might begin as early as late March, but it is more likely to occur in mid-April. This inshore movement may continue until late May during cooler spring seasons. Those few anglers who get in on this near-shore perch fishing each year believe these are pre-spawn perch; yellow perch are known to spawn at temperatures anywhere from 45 to 52 degrees.

This shoreline perch run is mainly confined to the evening hours, but sometimes schools will show up along the shallows earlier in the afternoon. With a gentle chop on the water and water clarity good but not quite clear, perch will move into these shallow areas in search of minnows, aquatic insects and snails.

Minnows, the prime perch bait in Lake Erie, get an even stronger nod when the perch are close to shore.

Tackle can be either simple or somewhat fancier. A fly rod, if used, should be long enough so that line need not be reeled when a fish is hooked. When a perch is caught, it is simply hauled tuna fashion onto shore. Then the line is fixed with another bait and set back into the water. No real casting is necessary and only the slightest of weight is used. Ideally, a small split shot and a pair of leadered hooks off the main line is all the terminal tackle necessary. Unlike still fishing for perch in deeper water, there is no need for colored beads and blades to attract fish into the area and hold them under the boat.

In this kind of fishing, the fish are either there or they must be found. The search is not usually a lengthy one. As the perch move toward shore with the lengthening of late afternoon shadows, they reach shoreline structures and begin moving along the outer edges. An electric trolling motor, either front mount or on the transom, does not disturb the fish as the boat is moving along these edges in search of perch. This silent approach will put the boat over fish more quickly. Once perch have been found, quietly drop anchor and see if they will hold under the boat.

Many yellow perch fishermen who have been sticking to deep water in mid-spring might be overlooking some fine action. When sunset is still an hour or more away, pull into a section of shoreline which has that same rock–and–gravel type of character where you'd expect to find bass later in the season. A bonanza of delicious perch fillets could be your reward.

Chapter 8

Late Spring Events

B lissful frustration marks the late-spring period (late May to early July) on Lake Erie—so many ways to fish for so many different kinds of fish. The problem aboard most fishing boats becomes finding room to carry all the necessary tackle items and finding time to use all that tackle.

Shoreline casting and shallow-water structure activity remain busy about the same time that the charter boaters and private offshore anglers start working the deeper structures—that suspended-level trolling activity that has made Lake Erie fishing nationally known.

As shoreline trollers gradually move farther away from shore, big schools of walleye cross paths with big smallmouth bass at various stages of spawning in the shallower waters. Suspended walleye get much attention as they lock into thermocline levels in search of high-protein forage baits—mainly smelt, alewives and gizzard shad.

While charter boats and privately owned boats—equipped with the latest downrigging and side planing tackle—run across stretches of deeper water, bass continue to work their way down the structures, striking voraciously at either live or artificial baits. Anglers skilled with vertical jigging techniques can easily connect with several species besides the popular walleye, namely bass, pike and big panfish.

Big Hits: Walleye and Bass

Walleye fishing can be as simple as casting a hand-held line with a plain jig to the most complex of lure combinations strung off either planer boards or downriggers. Walleye can be found cruising into the rocky shallows of the shoreline or sunken islands at dusk and just after nightfall. Or they can be hooked with live-bait rigs bumped along at medium depths (10-30 feet) while either drifting with the wind or trolling at a speed matching the metabolism of the fish as the water temperatures continue to rise.

In spring, walleye and panfish move into shore in the Western Basin, and fishermen move out onto the breakwaters to intercept them. Later, these same shore-based anglers will have a go at some smallmouth bass in these locations.

As early June arrives, walleye begin appearing in open-water areas all around the lake wherever large schools of baitfish can be found. Although there are no absolutes in the sport of fishing, efficient sonar equipment is almost an absolute necessity when seeking out suspended walleye in open waters. Rig fishing (planer boards/side planers and downriggers) will be covered in Chapters 11 and 12, but an understanding of schooling movements and early summer migrational patterns of walleye makes this kind of fishing more enjoyable.

Tradition has it that only certain reefs and shoals hold walleye during the late spring period, but Western Basin island-hoppers can attest to the fact that walleye will move over every shallow area likely to support forage. The trick here is to intercept fish as they are making their crossings.

Eastern Basin trollers work near shore, around shallow shoals, with floating minnow-type baits, to try and hook into these post-spawn walleye. In fact, all shoals, not just those near launch sites and large population areas, can hold impressive numbers of schooling walleye in relatively shallow water. A careful study of any good map of the lake shows many extended rocky points and long stretches of rubble rock. Many of these are untouched by daytime drifters casting weight-forward spinners or nighttime trollers hauling a floating stickbait along the shoreline. That is, many good walleye shoals in all basins of Lake Erie are overlooked in deference to the familiar and well-worked shoals.

The Michigan waters south of the Detroit River rarely reach depths of 25 feet. Trollers around Stony Point and the embayment west of the Toledo Harbor light are usually bypassed by casters and deep-water trollers heading out to work the deeper waters along the Michigan–Ohio borderline. Despite the relatively small amount of Lake Erie shoreline which exists in Michigan, a good many late-spring/early-summer walleye hang-outs can be found in these shallow waters.

There are two reasons for this largely overlooked fishing: (1) The fishing often occurs for only a brief time; and (2) The tradition of open-water casting has been an established method in the Toledo/Port

Clinton area for many years. After all, it was the weight-forward spinner cast from drifting boats in the Western Basin that first drew positive attention to the fantastic walleye fishery now gaining even more prominence for Lake Erie.

Ohio's reefs and islands in the Port Clinton/Catawba Island/Marblehead/Sandusky area support structures which draw crowds of fish and fishermen just after ice-out about the time that the walleye are entering their pre-spawn feeding cycle. But trolling—particularly in the nighttime shallows—has just recently started to catch on in the Western Basin. Most anglers would rather get on a party boat on a sunny, spring day and drift along as the boat moves into suspended schools of walleye in pursuit of bait fish.

Both Pennsylvania and New York suffer from late-spring "hot spotitis." The suffix "-itis" means an inflammation, and the Erie/Presque Isle area of Pennsylvania and the Buffalo Harbor area of New York becomes "inflamed" with shoreline trollers every spring. Yet rocky shoals west of both Erie and Buffalo support dozens of areas suitable for either casting or trolling for walleye. Once past Van Buren—at and west of Lake Erie State Park—a night troller may not encounter another boat until reaching Barcelona Harbor.

Sturgeon Point west of Buffalo and Sturgeon Bay west of Erie hold walleye schools only a few anglers pursue in late spring. Cattaraugus Creek and Dunkirk Harbor hold known spawning sites to the west at Silver Creek and Van Buren Bay, but active area fishermen rarely visit these sites either because they are not popular with the usual crowds or they are located some distance from public access fishing sites. Fishermen on Lake Erie tend to go with tried-and-proven locations. But walleye take up every useful site that might offer food and protection.

All in all, nighttime casting and trolling for walleye in shallow areas at the start of the spring season is almost as overlooked on Erie waters as the remarkable bass fishing.

Many Ways to Go

The alternatives open to anglers as June comes to a close are impressive. The first catches consist of post-spawn bass around shoals.

At the same time, walleye begin staging along the near-shore shoals and they relate mainly to bottom structures. Suspended walleye are moving away from shore in pursuit of larger bait fish which school well off the lake's bottom. For anglers who prefer walking to boating, bass movements in tributaries bring many to the shoreline at this time of year. Finally, yellow perch begin schooling in deeper water.

Late spring offers all of these possibilities, but with one catch: movements of these fish aren't as precise and predictable as the written word would make them appear.

Given that bass spawn with the moon phases, and that water temperatures must rise to somewhere above 60 degrees, no two spring seasons will offer the same date for post-spawn bass action to begin.

Walleye in the shallows remains something of a mystery to many

Some winners at a recent Lake Erie International (LEI) tournament show off the kind of quality and variety the big lake can offer up. Shown here are a 25–pound chinook, a 15–pound rainbow, a 10–pound walleye and a smallie that almost hit five pounds. Is the perch on the man's t–shirt?

Lake Erie fishermen. Any inland-lake walleye fishermen would beat the shore to a frenzy in search of weedline or rocky shoal areas holding walleye. Yet Lake Erie only sees a flourish of night trollers and the occasional drifter working into the shallows. Most boaters head out to deeper water once shore temperatures rise above 60 degrees. Most waders head up feeder streams in search of other species.

Suspended walleye has become such an attraction on Lake Erie that many fishermen don't get out until the first good reports of walleye taken on planer boards. But experienced board runners such as the charter captain team of brothers Lou and Walter Will run these boards at night from the beginning of walleye season in New York State. The Will brothers affirm that every major feeder is a trolling lane for planer boards as soon as walleye come off the spawning beds. By late-spring, walleye are still holding at the outside of shallow shoals and can be caught either suspended or belly to the bottom.

Bass fishing in lower stretches of feeder streams is a fact known to but a few. Most believe the only bass that go up creeks are the runts. Try a tributary some warm, late-spring morning with a spinner or shallow crankbait in places where steelhead were "hot" a month or two earlier. This fishery is not just for kids anymore.

Perch, most popular yet least known late-spring species, will be a bonanza one year and go bust the next. The best approach is simply to give them a try when heading out for bass, walleye or other species. If perch show up on the sonar and seem tightly schooled, drop in a light jig or jig-and-minnow to see if they are active. A fishing guide could make a respectable living if he were able to predict feeding patterns for late-spring, early-summer perch schools.

Clearly, with all these options available at once, most fishermen are forced to concentrate on only one or two. There's a lot of water to cover out there.

Rethinking Western Basin Basics

One late-spring trip to any port on or around the famed islands of the Western Basin will convince the observer that these waters have to be highly productive. Wide-beamed drift boats and lengthy cruiser-type vessels are tied off on every available length of dock space.

At this writing, chartering licenses for this area number slightly less than 800. True, many of the captains of these are "weekenders" who charter part-time or who are retired persons going out at their leisure. But many boats are run by young, energetic captains whose entire income is derived from chartering.

Interested fishermen should contact a local Chamber of Commerce for specific information on where charters dock. There are so many competent and energetic charter captains in the Western Basin that deciding on one often seems as complicated as the many good fishing options available at this time.

Most seasoned fishermen like to think that they are on top of their sport, tackle and techniques. Yet, there is always something more to be learned. The most basic of all tackle items in the Western Basin of Lake Erie for more than a decade has been the weight-forward spinner designed mainly for casting and sometimes drifting. Large companies as well as home-town lure makers are responsible for putting forth hundreds of cards with thousands of these spinner-and-worm rigs each spring. Each fall, most of the lures have been put to effective use in catching walleye somewhere in the Western Basin of Lake Erie sometime during the course of the spring and summer season.

Fred Snyder, District Specialist with the Ohio Sea Grant Program, estimates that 90 percent of the walleye caught in the waters north of the Toledo to Sandusky area are taken by casters sending out the standard spinner-and-worm suspension rig that has been so successful since walleye fishermen first discovered that walleye chase schools of minnows moving at depths well above bottom structures. As good as this combo might be, Snyder further asserts, there remain times when other things work better. In mid-summer, for example, there are occasions when the most seasoned head boat captain will not make contact with worthwhile schools of walleye when using spinner-and-worm rigs. Then, other ploys have to be tried.

At times, controlled planer board trolling and shallow-depth downrigging account for good—sometimes better—catches than the tried–and–proven weight forward spinner–and–worm rigs. It happens.

Success in the shallow, sometimes temperamental waters of the

Western Basin—in late spring and thereafter—depends much on a willingness to learn the basics, which means how to work weight forward spinners effectively. At the same time, there must be some flexibility and willingness to adapt to changing conditions. Studies indicate that Lake Erie's walleye population is fairly stable and that there are approximately the same number of adult walleye in each of the three basins of the lake. Each season, however, differs in regard to springtime water temperatures, bait movements, water clarity, wind direction, and so on.

As in the deeper waters of the Eastern Basin, there are no 100% surefire hot spots during late spring in the Western Basin. Late spring fish-finding calls for both knowledge and flexibility if the angler is to hit into the big numbers of bass, walleye, perch and other panfish that await at this time of year.

Chapter 9

When Bass Bust Loose

They populate Lake Erie's waters by the millions. Most of them die of old age. They often take a back seat to walleye and assorted species of salmonids. They require only modest management from fisheries departments. They have persisted in great numbers in Lake Erie through its most pristine days and its most pollution-ridden days.

Several years ago a lake freighter, heading toward Buffalo Harbor, ran aground of the beach at Sherkston, Ontario. An "artist" climbed aboard the wreck one summer and painted in bold letters on the rusted hull, "Lake Erie is full of ___." More accurately, the graffiti artist could have proclaimed, "Lake Erie is full of bass." Smallmouth black bass to be exact.

Lake Erie's smallmouth potential is on a par with that of its much better known walleye, perch and salmonid fisheries. However, even after several nationally-broadcast fishing programs and a major fishing tournament, bass are still a fairly well-kept secret among area anglers.

Paradoxically, one reason for the meager status of the bass in Lake Erie might be its very availability. The smallmouth fishing has always been there through periods of bounty and blight. It may just be a species that is taken for granted. Another possible reason may be the food fishing tradition that has always reigned in Erie. With so many good eating fish found here—yellow perch and walleye included—the bass (good eating, but not as good as those other two) was a ways down on the totem pole. It may have taken the great rise in pure recreational fishing, in modern times, to jettison the bass into somewhat greater prominence.

About Bass Spawning Cycles

Take it, as you will, as sound advice or simply folklore: bass spawning is controlled by moon phases, with water temperature and increased hours of daylight serving as additional factors.

If this moon-phase theory has merit, some early-summer seasons may not see the bass spawning cycle completed until sometime in early July—well after the official opener in all of the shoreline waters of the United States. When late spawning conditions prevail, it might be better to concentrate on the heavy schools of big panfish or the larger gamefish (walleye in particular) that have already completed spawning and are ready to take on baits set before them by nature and well-prepared anglers.

Tournament Talk

Major bass tournaments have recently called attention to the exceptional bass fishing possible for professional, competitive and everyday anglers. Operation Bass held its Red Man All-American Tournament at Buffalo in 1990, and the results confirmed what most close observers expected: large numbers of smallmouth bass and increases in the largemouth bass population (still not large enough to figure heavily in the contests). Tourney contestants also found out about Lake Erie's unpredictable weather.

Smallies provide all the action bass competitors can handle. All of

A raft of powerful bass boats revs up in preparation for the start of a major bass tournament on Lake Erie. The event was staged at Buffalo Harbor, but several of the contestants took their rigs as much as 50 miles down the shoreline seeking the poundage they needed to win.

the 41 finalists in the Red Man tournament felt smallmouths here to be tricky fighters. Having spent most of their tournament time in search of largemouth bass, which usually weigh in heavier than smallmouths, these seasoned experts from all over the United States came to Lake Erie waters and found that smallmouths both out-number and outweigh the Erie largemouths.

It wasn't long before tournament competitors were switching from either six- or eight-pound test line to ten-pound test. The heavier lines used for largemouth were too stiff and slowed the action of jigs and crankbaits; the lighter lines usually used in open-water bass fishing were too light to keep smallies hooked and quickly get them into the boat. The short period of fish fighting is needed so that the fish stands a better chance of survival and, after weigh-in, subsequent release.

The tricky part of tournament bass fishing lies in both finding them and then trying to bring them into the boat. Largemouths inhabit shallow, relatively quiet, stained waters. Smallmouths move to greater depths, can take moving currents and can survive well in relatively clear water. Yet another notable feature of smallies is their spectacular display of leaping ability once hooked. Tournament competitors all remarked that the smallmouth has an uncanny ability to shake the hook. Their acrobatics when first hooked call for quick responses. These tournament specialists had to compensate with tighter lines and more elaborate fish-fighting techniques. According to tournament rules, entrants may not use landing nets when boating their catch. Hence, these bass contestants were given some stiff tasks when faced with landing these Lake Erie smallmouths. Each fish had to be fought to a point where it could be lifted into the boat either with the rod or by hand. Yet the fish couldn't be so exhausted that it would expire in the live well.

As with everyday sport fishermen who get onto Lake Erie's open waters, the Operation Bass finalists were made to work their way through rough seas one day and farm-pond-calm conditions the next day. The final day of competition began with winds so powerful that tournament officials made the decision to hold the competition within the confines of Buffalo Harbor and the Niagara River.

The results showed area fishermen just how many bass—largemouth and smallmouth—could be found in the "off" sections of the lake. When Joe Thomas checked in with a limit of smallmouth bass in the 2- to 4-pound weight class at the end of the final day, his winnings came to $100,000. His fish were all taken in the most adverse of fishing weather: high winds, big swells and muddied waters. The top 10 finalists took home a total of $150,000, but the biggest winner was the fishery. Tournament results confirmed that good fish are there, and that good bass fishermen can catch them.

The future of the bass in Lake Erie looks bright. Further, as waters become even cleaner, it's possible that largemouth bass may increase in number and become a more important component of the overall bass catch.

Post-Spawn Pleasures

Early summer finds smallmouth bass abundant and fairly close to shore where almost anyone can catch them, but best techniques vary from area to area. Waters warm differently in the shallows of the Western Basin than in the deeper waters of the Eastern Basin, and this can somewhat affect methodology. Full-length books have been written and dozens of hours of instructional videos have been made on the ways to tempt bass, but the single most effective approach in that late spring to early summer period is "exciter fishing." What you want to do is simply get something in their way that triggers a strike. Later in the season, many live bait items will outperform lures, but post-spawn smallies seem to be spoiling for a lure at which to strike.

Exactly what will trigger a bass at any given moment is the big question. The expert bass angler, in these situations, will come up with an answer while the neophyte gropes. Mid-running crankbaits, metal- and foam-bodied spinners, spinner baits, wobbling spoons and any jig that can be cast and retrieved laterally will bring a smallmouth to the surface. Many believe that lures which simulate something which might threaten a spawning nest will touch off the dynamite—even when the nest is abandoned and the fish are well past the spawning cycle. Many bass experts believe that even beyond spawning, bass retain that protective instinct. The result can be powerful strikes at passing lures, even when the bass are not necessarily in a feeding mode.

Fisheries management agencies impose seasonal controls to protect bass during their spawning cycle. Generally, bass are protected (season is closed) until mid June. By that time, biologists believe most spawning has taken place and the fish have left the spawning beds. The Commonwealth of Pennsylvania changed its regulations for bass fishing beginning in the 1991 season. The new regulations eliminate possession of bass during the spawning season. Previously, anglers could take a two-fish limit (reduced from six bass) during the designated spawning period—March 15 to the third Saturday in June.

A word on conservation is needed here: even though states do not impose laws against catching and releasing spawning bass (and other species of catchable fish), try to avoid known spawning beds holding

FRED SNYDER / OHIO SEA GRANT

bass engaged in phases of spawning. Once the bass eggs are set and the fry begins to emerge from the bottom, nature can usually produce a healthy year class. But while the fish are spawning, most concerned bass fishermen try not to disturb these fish for fear of injuring them or interfering with their procreation.

When both the male and the female bass finish spawning, they feed voraciously. They will move up and down the shoreline in search of food to compensate for a long period without feed while spawning. During the spawning phase, vicious strikes usually come from fish still spawning and attempting to protect their nesting area. In clear water the spawning sites are often visible.

Popular Lures

The real fun begins when the fish have completed their spawning cycle and are feeding heavily. Anglers swear by certain lures which they consider patent bass catchers during the opener: light jigs, spinners, spinnerbaits, shallow-running crankbaits, poppers or floating minnow-type lures. But the truth is that any high-visibility artificial lure will work in the shallows for post-spawn smallies.

Black jigs work well because they contrast with the bright surface which bass see from below. Also, the rising and falling action of a lead-head jig closely represents crayfish, a principal forage item along stretches of rocky shoals which line much of Lake Erie's shoreline.

Spinners give off vibrations to attract bass. Most modern spinners have designs which allow them to turn at either slow or high speeds of retrieval, so the caster can adjust to the speed at which the fish are hitting. Spinner blades vary in shape from the long and narrow willowleaf to the rounded oval Colorado blade. Each different blade design sends out its own particular sounds, and spinner experts change blade shapes continually in order to find out what's working.

Spinnerbaits combine the provocative drop-lift-drop action of a jig with the sonic feature of a spinner. When retrieved along the surface, spinnerbaits also give off their gurgling sounds as they ripple along the water. When brought across either weeds or open water with weedless bottoms, a spinnerbait can bring up Lake Erie smallmouths in remarkable numbers. Because most smallmouth fishing takes place over rocky shoals and reefs in open water with no weed growth, spinnerbaits are mainly confined to subsurface use; subsurface here means close to the bottom. Buzzing a spinnerbait along the surface comes into play well after sunset on calm nights when bass are pushing bait schools into the shallows. During daylight hours, bass anglers would do better casting crankbaits.

Floater-diver crankbaits do it all: simulate bass food, wobble with an attractive motion and stay high where bass can see and strike them. They dig deeper when retrieved with either a sweep of the rod tip or a faster crank on the reel handle. They rise to the surface and float when the retrieve stops, thwarting foul-ups. Usually, the speed and manner of retrieve are significant, and varying combinations should be experimented with.

Lengthy debate begins when the subject of lure size is broached. The average angler sticks with mid-sized baits (#9 Shad Rap, K8

Kwikfish, Kill'r B2, A15 Bomber, etc.). But the devoted crankbait user will also keep an assortment of small baits (Wee Warts, Pee Wees, etc.) and also a complement of magnums in either the stick-type or rounded (alphabet) bodies (Magnum A, #11 or #13 Rapalas, Bomber 15A, etc.)

Poppers are confined to low-wind periods, usually sunrise and sunset. When conditions allow the casting of poppers, especially with fly rods, the angler can experience a quiet kind of fishing that reminds one of bygone days. The violent surface strike of a bass to a well-presented popper further enhances the experience.

Floating, minnow-type lures are the workhorse of Lake Erie shallow water bass fishermen. Typified by the Rapala or Rebel, this type of lure offers the considerable advantage of being both trollable and castable. Like crankbaits, minnow-type lures float to the surface when retrieval slows and dig toward the bottom with increased retrieval or trolling speed. In a true, match-the-hatch scenario, minnows make up the bulk of post-spawn bass forage and that's why minnow-type lures work so well.

Tracking Bass as Summer Advances

Tracking is not just for hunters of game. Gamefish like the bass can lead anglers on a chase that often sees the bass keeping one step ahead. While early-season bass fishing can be hot, heavy and handsomely rewarding, it doesn't take long before bass start moving away from their shallow haunts and begin to reduce their food intake somewhat.

After the bass action slows in the shallows, many anglers simply switch bases and go after the abundant walleye. Some also switch to perch, which may hold in tight schools the summer long. If walleye and perch are not options you wish to pursue, and bass remains your devotion, you'll probably have to do some hunting. Drifting for bass is possible, but connecting this way can take time, since the deeper bass-holding structures are not easy to pinpoint.

The hunt can go as deep as 45 feet in some rock-bottomed areas of the lake. The search is complicated by abundant schools of smelt which draw some of the bigger bass away from bottom once the crayfish population has been reduced. These big bass often are caught by downrig trollers running lures at suspended depths as they seek out walleye, trout and salmon.

Serious Lake Erie bass fishermen often switch to large minnows or small chubs to bring bass up from the deeper structures such as drop-offs. These large minnows can be presented either while anchored or slowly drifting on a low-wind day. Or, the big minnow can be moved along slowly with an electric trolling motor, on days when the waves aren't too high. This is not simply a minnow-dunking method. It is highly specialized and requires as much skill as is called for in controlled flip casting or ultralight jigging around weeds. Regrettably, sheepshead will sometimes take these big minnows when they're fished 20-45 feet deep, but at least this annoyance will be less than it usually is when fishing with soft-shelled crayfish in shallower waters.

Unless bass can be specifically identified in suspension on the sonar screen, begin the deep-structure smallmouth hunt along rocky bottom configurations, occasionally giving the minnow a gentle sweep upward and slowly lowering the rod tip to let the minnow dig for the bottom. Hits usually come as nothing more than light taps, and when to set the hook depends on how aggressively the bass are feeding at the moment.

Vertical jigging can sometimes take these deep-running bass, though vertical jigging in Erie waters is generally more productive on walleye and bigger perch. When the right wind conditions occur (low, steady winds with just a mild chop on the water—preferably the same direction as the drift), jigging Rapalas, Swedish Pimples and leadhead jigs can sometimes shine as bass fish finders in deep water.

Fishing for bass in deep water of course requires a boat, and is not as simple as shallow water bassing. Nonetheless, for those dedicated bass chasers, it is a viable alternative and provides a true test of one's boating and angling skills.

Chapter 10

Early Summer Panfisheries

Piers, docks and breakwaters offer anglers inexpensive and often fruitful ways to enjoy Erie's prodigality of panfish options. Somehow, fishing for perch, rock bass, white perch, calico bass, white bass and other relatively small critters has been universally associated with "kid fishing." These species, although good fighters on light tackle and great eating when cleaned and cooked properly, have been relegated to a position lower than what they merit. If by chance you've been overwhelmed lately by the intrusion of technology into fishing, then a day spent on the panfish grounds may be just what you need.

Trophy-hunting fishermen all but overlook the tremendous panfisheries found along Erie's shoreline. In fact, even the lowly sheepshead can put up a plucky fight when fought with an ultralight rod strung with four or six pound test line. And these and some other panfish grow to very healthy sizes here.

Schools of yellow perch averaging 10 inches in length and three-fourths to one pound in weight frequent Lake Erie's shoreline. But the heaviest buckets go to those anglers willing to move around and experiment with rigs and baits.

Perch are not generally regulated by season or creel numbers in most states on Lake Erie, although there is a 50-fish limit of panfish in the Commonwealth of Pennsylvania. But just because the season is year-round doesn't mean the fishing is easy year-round. Oversized panfish move both in and away from shore according to spawning patterns, available foods and other factors. Also, movements of perch predators can push these fish into and away from shoreline locations at unpredictable times.

In general, the best way to start is slowly. After ice-out, panfish might be found along most shorelines within easy casting distance of piers, docks and breakwaters, but water temperatures will likely keep their feeding activity constrained. Perch will take the bait, but they will probably not chase a fast-moving spinner, jig or minnow-type lure. Instead, the bread-and-butter rig of shoreline panfishing is a baited hook (or hooks) on a snelled leader held in place with a stabilizing sinker.

When perch feed in large schools close to shore, the biggest problem is getting fish off the hook and the line back into the water as quickly as possible. However, when the fish are scattered along the shoreline and not actively feeding, delicate tackle is sometimes needed. Many minnow dunkers our for perch fix small bells on rod tips or use ultralight lines and rods in order to detect fish when they're biting ever so lightly. Even the largest panfish, by the way, can get into this coy mood from time to time.

Lacking the mobility that boaters enjoy, shore casters are faced with adapting to such things as fish vacating a stretch of shoreline. At times, the task is as simple as moving along the shore to a position where eddies and currents have shifted, winds have pushed oxygenated waters shoreward or sunlight and shade patterns have shifted.

Other strategies relate to tackle, such as the widening of distances between snelled hooks, or adding spinners, "flickers" or colored foam beads as attracters. Finally, minnow size becomes critically important. Bait too big or small may mean the difference between an

empty bucket and one full of fish.

Big perch, for example, will often go for bigger minnows after ice-out and during the early weeks of spring. The popular reasoning here is that through the fall and winter seasons larger fish have depleted the numbers of smaller minnows and now what remains is mainly the larger, breeding-sized minnows. Thus while it might seem that small bait should be used to start the season in early spring, that turns out to not necessarily be the case.

Boating Bounty

Once the ice has cleared from the lake's surface, boating makes the search for perch even more interesting. As the perch begin moving away from near-shore sites and start settling over drop-offs and other bottom structures holding forage, the greatest challenge comes in trying to decide exactly where to fish.

Fishermen on big lakes are drawn to other fishermen, and nowhere is that principle more in force than on the Lake Erie perch grounds.

And, just as Lake Erie perch anglers group together they also tend to move together. There is nothing inherently right or wrong with this approach to stillfishing. Even with the advantage of preset Loran coordinates, the job can be a difficult one. Perch will often move away from a known position and seem impossible to find a day or two later. Electronics can take us to specific locations over wide expanses of otherwise unmarked waters, but the best piece of fish-finding equipment continues to be our sense of the situation at hand.

Early summer draws many Lake Erie anglers to the fabulous walleye fishing and opening of the smallmouth season accounts for still another large segment of the boating population. However, many devoted perch anglers stick with the larger schools and try to follow their migrational patterns as they steadily move away from shore during early summer's advancing heat. From Port Clinton to Lorain to Geneva to Hanover to Sturgeon Point (and a multitude of access sites between those points) there are resident anglers who take vacations to coincide with the best summertime perch fishing.

At Geneva in early July, for example, first-light perchers will be observed heading out to 30– or 40–foot-deep structures both west and east of the new launch site at Geneva State Park. It's not until an hour after sunrise that walleye trollers finally outnumber these perch devotees. Much of the Central Basin shoreline structure consists of rock, gravel and sandy drop-offs near shore (one to two miles out) ending at wide expanses of 60 to 75–foot–deep mud flats which extend across the lake to the shoreline structures along the Canadian shoreline. It's along the outer edges of these shoreline structures that early summer perch fishermen gather to work the bottom. Let's say it's July, and you've just dropped into a bait and tackle shop to buy a bucket of minnows and ask where the perch can be found. The answer might well be a precise number like 36, 40, or 42 feet. And the fish may hold at a specific depth for two or more weeks, depending on water temperatures and available forage.

Perch fishing in the deeper waters of the Eastern Basin is a slightly different story out of Cattaraugus and Sturgeon Point. Situated along drop-offs which lead to depths greater than 100 feet in places, the perch-holding structures can be somewhat more challenging. The search for perch may take boaters out to depths of 50–60 feet early in the summer season. It is during these early stages of deep-water perch fishing that Loran waypoints become useful.

One distinctly nice aspect of early summer fishing for perch in deeper waters is that the good fishing normally lasts through the entire day. Serious devotees will be out there at the crack of dawn, but many a boat load of buddies never drop anchor until 10 a.m. or later. It's entirely possible to head out after a late breakfast and catch more perch than you really want to clean well before dinner time.

Bait options are many. While minnows take a good number of perch at this time of year, there are times when perch show up on the sonar screen but don't show up on the hook. This is when alternative baits like worms, small nightcrawlers, oak-leaf grubs and hellgrammites can come into play. Another live bait that has become popular with both walleye and perch fishermen on Lake Erie in recent years has been the leech—not the blood suckers but the black variety sold in bait stores. These tough creatures hold up well when the perch are

While the men are out trolling for walleye, these ladies brave a rainy but warm day at the Mazurik Access Area. The goal: A bucket or two full of the white bass that this angler is showing to the camera.

hitting hard; it's not unusual to take 10 or 12 perch on one leech before having to replace it with a new one.

The Other Panfish

While perch are the number one panfish everywhere on Lake Erie, several others school well enough to become the object of an outing. White perch can be found among and above yellow perch in deeper waters. Often, when the yellow perch have turned off, the problem can be heavy numbers of white perch moving through the area. The trick here is to find out how high they are above the bottom. While perch fishermen typically set rigs within inches of the bottom for yellow perch, they sometimes miss the good numbers of white perch which move just a few feet off the bottom.

Bait and terminal rigs are essentially the same as those used for yellow perch, with the exception that the line has to be raised and lowered to the depth at which the fish are moving. As mentioned elsewhere in this book, white perch can provide some good eating when stored properly and prepared as soon as possible after the fishing trip has ended.

White bass, whose unwanted hits can also prove an aggravation to walleye and black bass pursuers, can nonetheless be fun to catch. These fish push large schools of baitfish to the surface and into shallow areas near shore. On a calm evening the surface can boil with scattering baitfish as the white bass move on through. Anglers on shore and in small boats move up and down the shoreline and cast small spinners and spoons into and along the sides of these boils for some fast action. The trick is to keep the lure near the surface and moving through the baitfish at the speed which best simulates a wounded baitfish. Little Cleos, Wobble Rites, Jig–A–Whopper, Mepps or Super Vibrax Spinners (in the 1/4–ounce sizes) all take their share of these fast feeders. Color is not nearly as important as a silver or chrome finish on at least half the lure; the silvery flash of a lure seems to turn these fish on. White bass will sometimes follow the lure to within a few feet of the boat and strike just as the lure is lifted for the next cast. It's a good idea to stop for a second or two at the end of a retrieve and give the lure a vertical jigging motion comparable to that used when ice fishing.

Crappies, though rarely found in open water areas of the lake, sometimes school heavily in bays and wide channels leading into the lake. Like the white bass, crappies tend to chase bait at suspended levels. When early summer approaches, these fish move great distances in search of bait schools. They may be found in one area at midmorning and then be totally gone a short while later. One of the best crappie presentation systems is the one used by professional bass anglers: front-mounted electric trolling motor, fan casting along likely weed and stump areas, and limited anchoring. Crappie fishermen differ from bass pros in that they use live bait and usually cast with light pencil bobbers. One highly effective way to find these nomadic panfish is to hook the minnow through the lips or head area and continually retrieve at a slow pace so that the minnow covers a wide area in a twitching, injured-minnow fashion. Toledo Bay, Sandusky Bay, Lorain Harbor, Presque Isle Bay, Dunkirk Harbor, Buffalo Harbor and several other bays, harbors and river mouths hold resident crappie populations. The task is to continually relocate them as they range over the shallows in search of their forage.

Catfish are yet another neglected resource in Lake Erie waters. While bullhead vacate shoreline areas in early summer, catfish will hold in the shallows throughout June and July. They can be taken in fair numbers and good sizes on those nights just after a heavy storm. When the wind has stirred and muddied shoreline waters, the cats move into shallow water virtually everywhere. Piers and breakwaters are good places to sit when tending lines, but long stretches of beach or rocky points work just as well. Heavy lines and sturdy tackle are in order here. These "panfish" sometimes exceed 20 pounds and simply swim away with little warning. Unlike the leaping bass and trout which often strike energetically, a cat picks up the bait and the next thing you might hear is a rod and reel plunking into the water. The best setup is similar to the one used for big salmon: once the line is cast and drawn tight, loosen the drag setting to very light and then set the clicker mechanism so that it signals a pickup.

Catfish baits are legendary. Most people have heard of the homemade cheese and blood concoctions so popular with catfish catchers.

Lake Erie summer catfishermen also go to large chubs (the size used for northern pike) and sections of chicken wings.

No fish here gets less respect than the sheepshead, the Rodney Dangerfield of Lake Erie finfish. It's a rare person here who admits to going out specifically for a bucket of sheepshead (fresh water drum). Yet many can be seen in or on pails, stringers, and fish baskets, particularly in Michigan and Ohio. Drum are caught along docks, piers, and breakwaters all summer long. Once considered strictly a bottom feeder, sheepies have been taken on downriggers set 70 feet down in 140 feet of water. Although they usually show up when hooks and lures are fixed with live bait, many "galvanized pike" have been taken with body baits and trolling spoons. Bob Lange, Great Lakes Fishery Coordinator for New York State, considers the sheepshead to be the most universally adaptable fish in Lake Erie waters. It can be found at all depths and levels, in seemingly any ambient water temperature. Like them or not, they are a fixture.

Anglers actively interested in taking these fish must have live bait. Minnows and crayfish do well, but nightcrawlers (the bigger the better) bring in the most sheepshead per outing. Boaters usually bump bottom as they drift along at slow speeds. Some, though, fish while at anchor. Shore based anglers keep their bait right on bottom with heavy sinkers.

The bad news (or good news, depending on your point of view) about these fish is that their numbers and sizes came down through the 1970's and 1980's. Once found in sizes exceeding 10 pounds and in good numbers, it is rare to catch sheepies today that weigh more than five pounds. Local taverns and marinas that hold "sheepshead tournaments" for laughs are sometimes surprised at the scarce numbers of fish turned in for prizes. It seems that as Lake Erie's waters have become less polluted, sheepshead have become less plentiful. Whatever the real causes are, the fact remains that sheepshead aren't as abundant as they were some 20 to 30 years ago.

Chapter 11

Plane and Fancy Boarding

The planer board is a relative newcomer to the waters of Lake Erie, but its rising popularity since the early 1980's has generated a new breed of fishermen—young and older innovators who tinker as much as they troll.

Anglers who wouldn't think of trolling with anything but a spinner and worm ten years earlier are fitting masts on the bow or sides of their boats and putting together both simple and more elaborate combinations of lures and electronics. Success with planer boards has caused crowding at launch sites from Monroe, Michigan, to Buffalo each summer. This chapter will look at the way in which the boards are effectively being put to use on Lake Erie.

Many Lake Erie regulars have commented that people who rarely buy costly fishing equipment start filling their boat with expensive toys once hooked on planer boarding. A Lake Erie troller/drifter in the 1950's would only have to make a modest investment for gear. No one would consider spending as much for surface-trolling gear as was

TYPICAL MID-SUMMER TEMPERATURE PROFILE

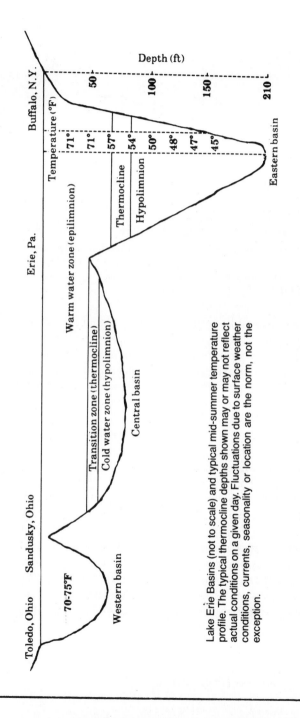

Lake Erie Basins (not to scale) and typical mid-summer temperature profile. The typical thermocline depths shown may or may not reflect actual conditions on a given day. Fluctuations due to surface weather conditions, currents, seasonality or location are the norm, not the exception.

Mark Damon of Jamestown proudly hoists the eleven pound wall-eye that took first prize in the 1990 Lake Erie International Derby. This trophy took a blue and chrome Bomber fished off a planer board in the waters off Barcelona.

spent for an outboard motor. When planer boarding first came into practice, most of the early planer rigs were designed and manufactured in the basements and garages of hundreds of homes around Lake Erie's shoreline. The cost factor was minimal. Today, modern manufacturers have greatly improved this type of equipment, but the price tag has correspondingly gone up.

Some will argue that all this fancy equipment has not increased the catch, but creel surveys prove otherwise. In fact, the planer board (and all side planing devices) remains the most effective tool yet devised for catching the larger Lake Erie walleye that suspend while searching for schools of bait fish.

Despite the proven effectiveness of planer boards, many trollers are reluctant to drill all those holes in the hull and carry along masts, containers of release clips and the boards themselves. Most established companies provide guides for line placement and rod configurations so that the multiple lines (usually two lines per man in most states on Lake Erie) can be handled without difficulties. Folding lure packs, hinged trays of suspended body baits and spoons and snap-on lure pouches let trollers see and get to lures without the classic tangle. The

Maxi-Mate tackle box, for example, stores approximately 200 spoons well within sight without tangling single or treble hooks.

Straight Talk: Lateral Lures

Trolling a long line behind a motor-driven boat as a means of triggering fish strikes is far from new. In fact, for many years this kind of trolling was routine.

With the development of better casting rods and reels, casting became more exciting and rewarding than either trolling of drifting. The idea of chugging back and forth over fish-holding areas of a lake became both monotonous and less effective than sending well-placed lures with modern casting equipment. In the hands of practiced casters, lures could be more effectively presented. Another generation of lures was designed to dive to calculated depths and offer a variety of motions plus sound and even scent to attract fish. All these innovations made casting a much more inviting option than the usual trolling techniques.

Another inherent problem with trolling is that most successful trollers were those who learned how to steer in arcs and controlled circles in order to work lures off to the side of the boat and away from the propeller blades. The popular wisdom has it that fish, especially suspended fish, are driven to either side of the boat as the trolling motor passes overhead.

Side turning, even properly executed, attracts only scattering schools of fish on one side of the boat per turn. Also, even with the most modern of sonar devices, the guy doing the steering could never tell just when the boat was coming onto a school and when a fish-attracting turn should be started.

Then came the side planer or planer board. Long an effective tackle item on Lake Ontario, where it was used on close-to-the-top salmon and trout, side planers gradually made their way onto Lake Erie. They were immediately put to use on the larger, suspended walleye. Fishermen were beginning to realize that walleye chase bait fish in much the same way as do the salmonids in Lake Ontario.

The basic principle of the side planer is simple: braced boards are designed to run either to the right side (starboard) or the left side (port) at a significant distance away from the boat. Special clips fixed with line-holding clamps (usually spring-loaded) are snapped onto the heavy line holding the boards. Once the boards are played out from one or both sides of the boat, a configuration of lures is set up so that the fisherman can quickly find out what lures are working.

After a desired length of line is let out from the reel, the line is then hooked into the clip or release and allowed to run off to the side a determined distance from the boat. The rod is then placed, usually in a vertical position, into a rod holder and the angler is free to set up other rod combinations with similar or differing lure presentations at varying distances from the boat.

The beauty of this system is obvious. The angler can set lines which run to both sides of the boat, thus placing lures in front of scattered fish on either side of the prop wash. With hands free to steer and set other lines, fishermen can try many more combinations than would be possible with a single, hand-held trolling rod. The more successful board operators are constantly changing colors, sizes, shapes and combinations of lures in order to determine what the fish are hitting on that particular day. The technique has made it much simpler for more fishermen to hook into the bigger fish that suspend during the warmer months of the year. To date, no other technique can more effectively get to and catch these bigger Lake Erie walleye.

With several line and lure combinations in the water, anglers can quickly determine lure depths and trolling speeds as well as preferred colors and sizes of fish in given schools. Trollers using a hand-held line and a rig fixed with only one or two lures worked directly behind the boat may take days to learn what a troller using side planers can discover in an hour or two.

Specific Planer Techniques

There are several tips and tricks that make these boards effective. Even though the side planer moves the lure well off to the side of the boat, controlled turning accounts for many more strikes than a lure drawn in a straight line along a fixed compass heading. When you develop an eye as to the way certain lures turn and track, strikes become more frequent. Knowing that a particular lure works better on a tight or wide turn is useful. Knowing effective trolling speeds for a particular lure can add to the count rapidly.

Side planing allows the freedom to experiment, but it remains up to the angler to keep making the observations and changes. Along with turning, careful attention to trolling speed can make all the difference in the number of strikes. Trolling speed indicators, therefore, are almost as important as sonar equipment. While no two speed indicators will be calibrated exactly alike, all you need do is relate the speeds on your unit to how your lures work and, ultimately, to what speeds produce strikes. Generally, for walleye the speed should be slower and for salmonids, faster. As a general rule, spoons can be trolled more slowly (1 to 2.5 MPH) and body baits (minnow-type plugs, diving crankbaits etc.) can be trolled faster (2 to 4 MPH—and sometimes faster).

The best judgement of lure speed, however, is still made by first-hand observation. As in all trolling situations, place the lure in the water and see how it runs or tracks at given speeds in given water conditions. If the lure shows good movement from side to side without spinning or hydroplaning toward the surface, the lure will probably take fish.

Finally, line length and lure weights become more important as the season progresses and the fish start stacking in deeper water farther from shore. Line lengths of 200 feet or more are not uncommon by mid-summer. In-line sinkers as heavy as four ounces set three or four feet ahead of the deepest diving crankbaits help the lure reach depths of 40-50 feet as it runs off to the side of the boat.

Fancy Patterns

The single biggest mistake most beginning side planers make is to load their equipment as though they were going for 30-pound salmon or 15-pound trout. Lines from 15 to 20-pound test will take walleye from Lake Erie, but eight- or ten-pound test quality monofilament is strong enough to bring fish into the boat and will be much less visible to the fish.

Along with lower visibility and reduced line drag, the lighter lines allow for more lure action at lower trolling speeds. Many salmon trollers on either Lake Michigan or Lake Ontario come to Erie only to first encounter limited strikes and fewer than expected walleye hook-ups. Often, the problem is equipment that is too heavy. It's only when they scale down that their expertise translates into walleye limits.

Heavy lines and shock-absorbing gear is not needed for most walleye taken in Lake Erie. For example, a "snubber" (a segment of flexible tubing used to ease the shock of heavy fish strikes) will often mask the presence of a "shaker" (a fish too small to pull the line from the release clip). Everyone hears stories of 10-pound-plus walleye ripping off line like a salmon or trout. But the greater need here is to detect shakers and get them off the line as soon as possible. When this occurs, two problems emerge: (1) the undersized fish on the line prevents larger, more desirable, fish from striking; and (2) the smaller fish is probably being drowned as it is dragged along undetected.

Light but not ultralight lines and releases can be set to trip with

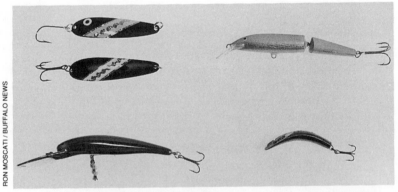

RON MOSCATI / BUFFALO NEWS

Four of the many ways trolling lures can be altered to increase effectiveness or action: Upper left, single hook usually lands more fish; upper right, jointed Rapala with belly hook removed; lower right, banana-type lure (here a Kwikfish) with belly hook removed; and lower left, Bomber 25A with belly hook altered. (Here, each hook in the treble has been clipped at its base and then a scent–saturated pipe cleaner has been affixed to the remaining shank.)

the strike of even a smaller fish. They make for more efficient and much more sportsmanlike fishing.

Releases exhibit varying degrees of complexity but every model has some sort of line-holding device that allows for the line to pull away from the release when a fish strikes. In order to detect the lightest of strikes, ones which sometimes fail to trip the release, place a loop of line through the jaws of the release clip so that the loop extends through the jaws and out the other side.

Many experts give the line three or four twists before placing the line inside the clip. This ploy accomplishes several things, specifically: (1) The crossed line tends to release more positively—it does not take a set in the vinyl/rubber pads; and (2) Smaller fish—ones too small to trip the release—will often pull the loop down to the release, closing against the release. When the loop disappears, the small shakers can be more readily detected and humanely released.

Another side planer trick is to set lures so that they run parallel to each other. First, keep track of the length of line sent out on each rod. Water clarity and wave action dictate proper distances behind the boat, but lure alignment helps in all wave and weather conditions. Each time a line is removed or added to a sequence set on one side of the boat, try to match the distances of the other lures. That is, outside lines will be shorter than inside lines (those closer to the boat), because the planer board and drag line are farther back in the water as the boat pulls them along. To keep the lures running together, the lines running inside will have to be longer than the outside lines. These side-by-side lure presentations increase the number of strikes and the number of fish boated.

Many trollers remove the belly hooks on some lures, a tip worth applying in almost all trolling situations. Cut off the belly hooks and replace the tail hook with one a size or two larger. Some lure designs are such that they need the weight of the belly hook to maintain balance and swim properly. If so, try snipping off the hooks at the base of the shank and leave the shank as a balance weight. Lynn Barnett, designer of the Barney's Schooler—a multiple-lure trolling device—points out that a few strikes are lost with the middle hook removed, but there is a greater percentage of fish caught once they are hooked and have set off the release. This hook surgery also reduces the fouling of lures in the landing net, and the possibility of catching a finger or hand in the other treble when removing hooks from a fish.

A "three-way" rig is yet another way to improve catches with planer boards. This rig consists of a body bait and spoon run on separate leaders. Tie two leaders on a three-way swivel in the following pattern: (1) A 54-inch leader with a deep-diving crankbait (Hot n'Tot, Bomber 15A or 25A, Bagley DB, Wiggle Wart, etc.) and (2) A 72-inch leader with a flutter spoon (Slammer, NK, Mod-U-Lure, Pirate, High-Tech, etc.). These leader lengths allow the bait to travel directly below the spoon and create a schooling effect.

A Little More on the Side

With all the intricacies of planer boarding, it would seem that there is enough tackle down there to attract every fish in the lake. Ironically, somewhere between the deepest set planer board line and the shallowest downrigger line lies a kind of dead zone. The proof is shown when anglers troll something in between the two rigs.

Dipsy Divers, Jet Divers, Hot Shots, Yellow Birds, and many other in-line planing devices have been around for years, but their successes with walleye on Lake Erie are just now becoming well known. The combination rigs with multiple leaders and the alternate side planers (not on a planer board line) pick up fish missed by lures on either downriggers or planer boards.

Of the many side planing devices in use on Lake Erie, Dipsy Divers have exceeded all others in getting to those hard-to-reach fish on the side of the boat. A simple disk with an adjustable release clip and weighted directional plane, the Dipsy can be set at precise depths and distances by a measure of line length and the setting of the directional weight. The combination of a Daiwa LC 47 reel on a Great Lakes System rod provides the line-counting needed to set the depth of the Dipsy. Daiwa has designed a series of rods specifically for the strong pull the Dipsy exerts as it moves to the side. Twenty-pound-test line is the recommended minimum line weight. Some trollers have gone to either wire or braided dacron line to add strength with less line drag when side planing the Dipsy. Trolling a Dipsy Diver makes hit detection fairly simple. Any change in the action of the arched rod is a fish. Powerful fish pop the rod tip and lighter fish shake or put a greater bend in the arch of the rod.

Straight diving devices (Jet Divers and Pink Ladies) run deep without requiring the placement of a lead weight ahead of the lure. With the right setting on planer board releases, these divers can be strung off planer board lines and set to dive 30 feet or deeper and well off to the side of the boat.

Yellow Birds, Hot Shots, and other clip-on small boards work best in gentle waves. High-rolling waves or sharp chops make these devices flip or dive. When waters are calm, Yellow Birds give precise visual sighting of side planers, and trip with ease when fish strike.

Regardless of distances and density of devices, what goes on the end of the line is still the main consideration. Before sending out any lure on any side planing device, check the lure's action as it trails the line-altering device behind which it is being drawn. The rigs set the lines, but the lures catch the fish.

If all these line combinations seem like they could turn into spaghetti, start out simply and decide which side-planing devices can work best for you. A couple of lines set off the side with opposing Dipsys may be all that's needed to limit out on walleye. The separation of the two side lines allows for a flat line or two to be sent out directly behind the boat. After developing a feel for how the lines plane and what your boat is capable of handling in the way of equipment items, the next step might include the complex masts, combination rigs and other, more elaborate, side planing additions. Despite the complexities, once they are effectively set up, boards catch fish.

Chapter 12

Up With Downriggers

"We can see them swimming under our boat!" the voice on the VHF radio exclaimed, "but we can't get them to hit." The problem was seeing big walleye moving through clear water only 10 to 15 feet below the sun-drenched, flat-calm water surface. The boaters stopped and cast jigs and crankbaits at them. No takers. They "stretched the boards" (let out more line from the planer boards) and went to floating-type lures. No strikes. Then they hit on the idea of dropping a downrigger weight to a controlled depth with a straight-running stickbait. After a few shallow settings were tried, walleye began hitting silver and blue lures at a depth of just 10 feet. More than 100 feet of line was let out before it was clipped to the release on the shallow-run rig weight. The secret was to get the line down but still keep it fairly shallow, where feeding walleye were willing to move even though most conditions were adverse: warm, flat-calm water; bright sunlight; and boat motors running directly overhead. No, this scene is not acted out every time a trolling rig is placed on a shallow setting, but it's an approach that sometimes works in

The transom of a boat set up for some comprehensive walleye trolling with either side planers or downriggers. Such a spread will keep all hands busy when a school of glasseyes is encountered.

either shallow or deep water when all other trolling methods fail.

Like side planer methodology, downrigging techniques came to Lake Erie from the trout and salmon filled waters of Lakes Michigan and Ontario. Sharp-eyed charter boat captains saw that big walleye were chasing bigger bait fish well away from the bottom structures of the lake.

Commercial fishermen had known for decades that they could set their gill nets at shallow depths over deep water—sometimes just below the surface of the water—and trap walleye during the day as well as at night. Historically, commercial netters had set nets at all depths when the lake was teeming with blue pike. Once that species began diminishing to less than profitable levels, they were forced to drop their nets near the bottom and harvest yellow perch. But, as the blue pike began disappearing, some netters started seeing larger and larger walleye appear in the small-meshed nets set for the smaller blue pike.

Sport fishermen began taking cues from the findings of these commercial netters. If the walleye were not consistently holding close to bottom and shoreline structures, new tackle would have to be invented to catch fish that chase suspended schools of bait fish.

Unlike the inland lakes of most midwestern states, Lake Erie walleye required specialized equipment; as it turns out, what worked was the same gear that had proven successful on trout and salmon in other Great Lakes. Knowing that the walleye—particularly in the Central and Eastern Basins of Lake Erie—live most of their adult lives in the upper reaches of the lake, at least during the warmer months of the year, fishermen hastened to apply downrigging techniques in ways similar to those used on trout and salmon.

The walleye here were not shallow enough for side planers or deep divers. But salmon trollers, who had long known that lures could be trolled just a few feet behind a downrigger weight or main cable, found that these short leaders did not consistently take Lake Erie walleye.

The first adaptation for lightweight downrigging had to be setting releases light enough to detect the lighter strikes of the walleye. Anyone who has been out salmon fishing on either Lake Michigan or Lake Ontario can attest to the devastating strike and phenomenal amount of line run off the reel's drag from even a modest-sized salmon. The problem with setting rigs for salmon is simply to keep the equipment on board during those critical first few seconds when the fish attempts to rip rod and reel out of the holding device.

Walleyes, on the other hand, strike a trolled lure much more lightly than either salmon or the larger bass. Many charter captains speculate that walleye swim along with the lure before and after being hooked. It is not uncommon to drag along a walleye as large as five pounds for a prolonged period of time without having a release or seeing a difference in the rod's arc as it rests in its holder. This can kill a fish that the angler might otherwise choose to release.

For purposes of both conservation and effective fishing, a careful system of release mechanisms is a must when fishing for suspended walleye with downrigger equipment—shallow or deep.

Since walleye often do not hit lures set close to the rigger weight one must let out more line, and this adds another complication—line stretch. Line used in downrigging should have a minimum of stretch, so that the fish will effectively trip the release mechanism.

There are yet a few other touches that can be applied when downrigging for walleye. First, reel up so that the rod has as much bend as possible and then back off on the drag to a point just short of where it would free spool. Then, set the clicker mechanism. At times, a click or two is all it takes to detect the strike of a "shaker."

As you would with a planer board release, put a twist in the line at the point where it's held in the pads of the release mechanism. This will allow the line to release more easily when a fish lightly tugs at the device. Downrig twists differ from planer board line twists in that the downrig line need not extend in a loop through the other side of the release. Also, downrigger sets take a few more twists than the one or two twists employed with planer board releases.

Lure color can sometimes be a big factor. Various tackle manufacturers now produce devices aimed at helping you to select the right color lure. Some of these units are hand-held while others have sensors that are attached to a downrigger weight. The readings indicate a main (dominant) color as well as side bands (alternatives) for possible lure colors.

When talking with rig fishermen on shore or listening to fish chatter on the VHF radio, one of the most frequent questions asked—after kind and color of lure used—is the length of line set between lure and release. Sometimes lures are clustered near the weight so that they might collectively serve as an attracter; at other times, these close setups have a negative effect. If the lure is set too close, walleye might not hit. If the lure is set too far back, line stretch might thwart proper releases. The trick is to strike just the right balance. How? This problem has more to do with adaptation than a specific technique. Constantly check your lines. Work out a system by which all lines are checked say at 15, 20 or 30 minute intervals.

Not only does a system like this afford the opportunity to change lure colors, but it also may serve to pick up fish moving above the downrigger setup. Experienced riggers never reel in a line immediately after they intentionally pop that line from the release. Instead, they allow the body bait or spoon to continue moving along as it is gradually drawn up toward the surface. Many strikes are garnered in this fashion.

When these near-surface hits occur, it is time to reconsider the settings of your downriggers. Novice and veteran downriggers alike tend to set rigs too deep for suspended walleyes. True, if the lines are set too high fish won't rise to strike the lures, and no contact will be made. But if the lure is below the fish and strikes only occur when line is released and the lure rises up towards the surface, it's a sure sign that the rigs should be brought up to a shallower setting.

There is no question that downriggers are, first and foremost, a means of getting deep with relatively light tackle and reasonably short line lengths. Ultimately, though, what depths you run at will be determined by where the walleye schools are, as told by your sonar screen or prior experience. Once you've made this assessment, set your rigger patterns so that some lures are a little below the fish and some are a little above.

Higher Still

Tackle tinkerers have devised systems to increase the number of lures that can be run off the same downrigger cable. Two of the more popular items are called "stackers" and "sliders."

A stacker is nothing more than an additional release clipped or snapped onto the cable at a determined height somewhere above the downrigger weight. The stacker allows the angler two or more additional lures on the same downrigger. The stacked line can be set so that it's ahead of, behind or at the same distance from the cable as the line set in the lower release. Experienced trollers with several fishermen on board will stack two or more lines above the rig weight, but the average angler, fishing with only one or two others, will be kept busy with two lines running on one line—and possibly another rig set with the additional stacker line.

Sliders, sometimes also called "cheaters", are short leaders fixed with a large swivel snap at one end (for attaching to a preset fishing line) and a smaller swivel snap at the other end (for attaching a selected lure). The slider is clipped onto either the regular downrig-

George Dovolos (left) and Ted Depczynski with a mixed bag of walleye and trout. These fish were all taken within a one–mile radius in the deep waters between Dunkirk and Barcelona Harbor. Although relatively few here fish expressly for salmonids, they are available for skillful anglers.

ger line or the stacked line and simply drops to a point where the line bows (usually half way down).

There is little depth control in the placement of sliders. Theoretically, it will be down half the distance of the line on which it is set. But currents, line drag, line stiffness and lure action all make for varied slider presentations.

What all these lure combinations offer is the creation of a bait-school effect, which the famous angler Seth Green understood and applied more than a century ago. Although the rig he put together was a hand-held one, it featured the stacking of leaders and trolling spoons. Green fished mainly for lake trout in the Finger Lakes, but the "Seth Green Rig" became well known beyond the borders of this region. All modern downriggers today enjoy increased catches as a result of Green's understanding of suspended bait schools and of the "excitement factor" created through the simultaneous use of several lures working closely together.

Weight and Seasons

Downriggers are not just for suspended fish. Nor do they have to be run at fixed depths. Rigs can be set with oscillating mechanisms which lift and drop the weight at controlled intervals. Rigs can also be coordinated with a sonar unit to maintain a fixed distance above the bottom.

Most rigger boats use the same size weights. But the more successful downriggers change weights as they run deeper or shallower. In Michigan waters shallower than 25 feet, most riggers run six-pound weights. Off Baracelona, a 15-pound weight is not a radical choice when trolling at depths greater than 100 feet. After the summer run of walleye, anglers who don't head upstream for the coho and steelhead take walleye as deep as 140 feet in the Eastern Basin. Heavier weights also keep multiple rigs in line and less likely to tangle; and help sliders and stackers to run straight so that they give more accurate readings of the depths at which the fish are hitting. Also, heavy weights hold combination rigs in line. Additional line drag occurs when running a spoon-and-plug combination or a rotating spreader with multiple spoons such as the Barney Schooler. The Schooler is a device which rotates two spoons so that at any given moment the bait appears disoriented and heading both up and down as it moves along.

It's true, many riggers simply watch the sonar readings and then move up or down to match the marks on the screen. But the real downrigger pros are constantly experimenting and adjusting their tactics to match changing conditions of all sorts. Watch a good captain or mate sometime as he works the rigs during a day's fishing. It's like watching an artist at work.

Chapter 13

The Niagara River and Head of the River

It could be called a lake within a lake. It has fast-moving currents, weed-lined backwaters, sunken-island structures, shoreline drop-offs, and wide expanses of mud and sandy bottom. This area, known as the Head Of The River, encompasses approximately five miles of Erie between the Canadian and U.S. shorelines. The Canadian shoreline extends west from Fort Erie to Windmill Point. The U.S. shoreline extends south from Buffalo to the mouth of Smokes Creek in Lackawana.

The waters at the head of the Niagara River—mainly on the U.S. side of the line—are known as the "Fish Market." Current is strongest here, where shallow shoals rise above the surface when water levels are low. Travellers crossing the Peace Bridge during the warmer months of the year can look upstream, towards the lake, and see a gathering of boats at almost every hour of the day or night. Boaters will often drift the Fish Market current at midday, when walleye aren't hitting anywhere else. Fish will actively feed in the current formed as Lake Erie enters the narrows of the upper Niagara River.

Donnelly's Wall, possibly the most familiar place name among Buffalo area fishermen, is the last visible man-made structure seen when entering the main current of the Niagara River. The wall attracts trollers, drifters and anchored casters, depending on the time of day and seasonal conditions. Fishermen can be seen day after day at Donnelly's, but boat traffic really jams the wall at and after sunset. Parallel to the wall are shifting currents caused by changes in wave height on Lake Erie; bait schools move in to feed along the outer edges of the currents. The waters slightly recede after sunset just enough to bring bait fish and walleye together along the wall.

The three major openings (known as "gaps") in the Buffalo Harbor breakwater create current diversions and eddies which hold schools of bait and a generous assortment of gamefish. This three-mile-long rock wall holds fish on both sides: the calm waters on the harbor (inner) side and the moving waters along its outer wall. Bass enthusiasts need motor no farther than the outer breakwaters of Buffalo Harbor for enough excitement to please everyone.

The Smokes Creek area takes in a two-mile-wide shoreline spawning area with a wide expanse of sunken islands and shallow shoals which hold bass and walleye for much of the warm-water fishing season. Boating activity around Smokes picks up once walleyes have finished spawning and begin their post-spawn search for food along the Town of Hamburg's shoreline shallows.

Waverly Shoal, the largest sunken-island structure in the Eastern Basin, is entirely in Canadian waters. Surrounded by mud flats with an average depth of 30 feet, this shoal is actually several sunken rock islands gradually rising to a 10-foot depth at the green buoy (#EU 3) at its extreme northern end. This shoal is ideal for drifting. When modest (5 to 10 MPH) winds move in from the west, boaters head upwind, line up with the channel buoy and drift over these varying structures for remarkable numbers of walleye, bass and good-sized perch.

Unlike the breakwater lined Buffalo Harbor and the shale cliffs along the U.S. shoreline, the Canadian shoreline is marked by jagged, granite walls, large boulder bluffs and gravel washes in many shallow-water areas. The shoreline is difficult to navigate, because of the many rock formations, several of which lie inches below the surface. Yet these shallow areas are precisely where much of the best bass fishing can be found. Prevailing winds push bait into these warm shallows for prolonged periods, which accounts for the respectable number and size of walleye, bass, perch, and even some good-sized northern pike taken here each year. Trolling, casting and drifting all account for good catches of walleye, smallmouth and perch during the warmer periods and fair numbers of trout and salmon when cooler weather arrives.

Returning to the head of the Niagara River, two distinct structures rise above the surface directly in the main current: the "Roundhouse" and the "Crib." The Roundhouse, a round, tile building serving as a water intake for the City of Buffalo, is clearly visible in U.S. waters. The Crib, much less visible and a potential hazard to navigation, is located along the western channel edge, dividing U.S. and Canadian waters. The area embracing these two structures forms a dividing line between the open waters of the lake and the moving currents of the fish market.

Because of the size of this area and variety of fishing experiences it has to offer, many anglers keep a boat moored at Buffalo's Small Boat Harbor and do not venture out either into Lake Erie proper for open-water walleye fishing or down the Niagara River for muskellunge, bass and trout fishing. There are enough options at the Head Of The River to keep a boater busy all season.

A Province of Ontario, as well as a New York State fishing license is recommended when fishing here. The international border is hard not to cross over from time to time, even with the best of maps and Loran coordinates. Having both licenses will save you from having to worry about it.

Species Timetables

Despite the well-publicized muskellunge activity that occurs around the Strawberry Island area of the upper Niagara River, the much more popular species at the Head Of The River are small-mouth bass and walleye. Depending on the time of year, the gradually building current of this area may attract bait schools which subsequently attract schools of feeding bass and walleye.

Bass are the first to become numerous, even though walleye typically "wake up" sooner in the spring. Bass move into these fast-moving waters and hold along the many shoals and shoreline edges once water temperatures reach 55 degrees. The post-spawn feeding and migrational movements of bass become even more pronounced once water temperatures reach 60 degrees. Good bass catches are made with the opening of bass season in June (third Saturday in New York State and fourth Saturday in the Province of Ontario waters). Given seasonally normal water temperatures, bronzebacks will hold along these shallows until late July before they head into the deeper waters.

Heavy walleye movements in the Head Of The River will begin well after the fish have spawned and gone through their post-spawn feeding frenzy. While walleye in most areas of either Lake Erie or the upper Niagara River become active feeders shortly after completing their spawning cycle, river experts don't look for good walleye runs until sometime in mid-August. Some walleye schools will move in and out of the harbor areas in early summer, but the really hot time extends from mid-September until the formation of ice.

Muskellunge activity in the Head Of The River is divided between the spring and fall seasons, with the greater numbers of trophy-sized muskies taken in late fall—just before ice forms.

Yellow perch schools can be found throughout the Head Of The River. Larger concentrations of perch, however, hold in the deeper Canadian waters (generally exceeding 30 feet) during that long period extending from mid-June to early September.

Techniques

Approaches are significantly dictated by currents and wave activity. Prevailing southwesterly winds push waves along the gradually shoaling waters. Either trolling or controlled drifting become necessary because of the steady movement of water. Boaters will anchor along shoreline edges or at points well into the lake, where currents are neither dangerous nor an impediment to holding an anchor.

Casting also has its place in these moving waters. First-light bass casters line up along the rock structures of Buffalo Harbor walls on calm, early-summer mornings and gradually drift downcurrent while casting crankbaits, jigs or live crayfish toward the boulders which form the protective wall.

Straight-line drifting—simply dropping a weighted line and drifting with the waves and or current—accounts for many bass, walleye and perch at all hours of the day. The popular three-way rig has gone through many a refinement in the hands of these upper river drifters. Weights can be as complex as tonsil or spoon-shaped "bottom walkers", or "chugging irons." A chugging iron is a 6- to 30-inch-long heavy brass wire with a lead weight fixed an inch or so below the ring formed at the top. The weight can be, simply, a spark plug, wheel weight or other discarded chunk of metal. Leaders vary in length, depending on orientation to the current, water clarity and species sought. In fast-moving, moderately stained waters, a short leader of two to three feet in length is possible. In clear, sunlit, nearly calm waters, a longer, finer leader will be less noticeable to wary fish feeding in the clear waters.

Trolling, possibly the most popular technique among regulars who fish the Head Of The River, calls for a familiarity with the location of shallow structures of all water levels and an ability to handle a boat in water currents which change quickly as they pass the many natural and man-made bottom features. Many area residents recall the difficulties the U.S. Corp. of Engineers had in removing a barge from the pilings of the Peace Bridge after the barge had been lost in heavy currents at the Head Of The River.

Lure presentation can become involved, because fish move over these shallow structures in fast-moving currents. The business of a troller is to find the lure which will run at the right depth and speed in these currents. Too shallow, and the lure passes over the fish; too deep, and the lure gets snagged and becomes a part of the bottom's structure. Popular shallow-running lures are Rapala's Floating Minnow, Storm's Thunderstick, Bomber's #14 or 15 Long A, Bagley's Bang-O-Lure, Rebel's Minnow or Fastrac, Cotton Cordell's Red Fin and other minnow-like floater-diver lures. Any one of these gives the appearance of a being a slender, injured minnow attempting to right itself and escape to the bottom.

These shallow-running lures need to be checked for depth of running and lure action, regardless of manufacturer's claims. For example, a lure which might be advertised as running at depths of five to eight feet may not in reality dive below four feet; however, this lure may work well anyway in extremely shallow, rocky shoals, where deeper-running lures would simply hang up on the rocks or scoop up bottom debris.

Deeper running lures, originally designed for casting to bass, have found their place in tackle boxes of trollers seeking fish at suspended or near-bottom depths. These lures, generally referred to as crankbaits, are best known to bass fishermen, but trollers—particularly those running in relatively shallow waters without weights attached to the line—began adapting these crankbaits for controlled-depth trolling.

Peak Periods

Several peak periods occur at the Head Of The River: late May for walleye, late June for smallies, and mid-summer for perch. But the ideal time of the year for a variety of fishing experiences might be mid to late October, when the water temperature is approximately 65 degrees. This is according to Ted Depczynski of Cheektowaga, veteran Head Of The River angler. Bigger smallmouth bass and muskies can be taken at this time, but walleye catches are the real news during this productive fall period.

Depczynski, with more trolling lures on board than can be found in many small tackle shops, has worked out elaborate systems of trolling all the waters affected by currents at the Head Of The River. He considers sundown till 10 p.m. the ideal time to connect with incoming schools of feeding walleye. Deep and shallow-running crankbaits are alternately used when making trolling passes from the deeper to the shallower waters. Boat placement is essential, with deeper lines set on the down side of a structure and shallow-running (short-lipped baits) on the higher side of the structure. Many walleye in a five-fish limit catch will weigh closer to ten than five pounds. While running these bigger trolling baits, Depczynski sometimes hooks into smallies weighing more than five pounds, as well as those monsters that cause all the excitement in the main

The upper Niagara River at the International Rail Bridge. Straw-berry Island, musky country, is seen as a small speck of white just below the tip of Grand Island. Photo by N.Y. Power Authority.

sections of the Niagara River: 20-pound-plus muskellunge.

Upper River Runs

The upper Niagara River offers the opportunity for several kinds of trophies, but the one with the larger than life reputation is the toothsome muskellunge. It spends much of its life in fast-moving current and feeds on the same fish most anglers are trying for: bass, walleye, trout, and panfish. Some musky men believe that there are subtle difference between the Niagara River muskies and those which swim in the waters of the St. Lawrence River or Chautauqua Lake. The sleek body and deep green coloration are not scientific proof of a subspecies, but river anglers see and note these features when they catch muskies in the Niagara.

Musky trollers can be seen up and down the river, but the focal point for trolling is the triangle formed as river waters move around the head of Grand Island. Upstream from Grand Island and at the center of this current is Strawberry Island, which creates backwaters and eddies. Trollers make passes east and west of Strawberry in the main current of the river, attempting to run big baits by the muskies as the fish hold along edges and wait for prey to be pushed to them in the current. While boaters may troll for hours, potential contact time with the fish will only last a few minutes on each pass. With currents too powerful for casting or drifting, a trolling motor is the best way to make controlled passes.

Niagara River musky fishing peaks at about the same time of the year as walleye fishing at the Head Of The River. Peak times of the day, however, differ considerably. While walleye runs occur at dusk and later, trophy muskies are out and feeding much of the day. Two seasoned river trollers, Mike Bordonaro and Tom Slomka, have seen days in October when the muskies move out from cover and hit bigger baits all day long. Flourishes occur an hour after sunrise and an hour or two before sunset, but fish will hit the well-presented lure whenever it arrives.

Bordonaro and Slomka collect all kinds of musky lures and have a high regard for Creek Chub's classic lure, the Pikie Minnow. However, Bagley's DBO 8 series has revolutionized musky fishing for many musky trollers in the upper Niagara River. Color on these big Bagleys can make a difference. Bordonaro prefers "Tennessee Shad", "Red Muskie", and "Mullet" finishes, because they most closely match bait in the river. Which specific finish is used depends on whether the water is clear or stained at the moment. While the Swim Whiz, Magnum Rapala, and Mirrolure work well on river muskies, the 8-inch Bagley has taken more than its share of trophy-sized muskellunge in recent years.

Muskies Incorporated, a small but devoted group of river fishermen, have long advocated catch-and-release of all fish that are not considered wall-mount candidates. Many devotees of this singular sport believe that excessive fishing pressure can in fact reduce the average size of muskellunge to well below trophy class. Whenever possible, release smaller muskies without removing them from the water.

Other Upper River Chances

Anglers not inclined to wrestling alligators next to the boat can still have fun on the upper river. Early spring and late fall walleye runs balance out late spring, early summer and mid-fall bass activities. Drifting the currents along Fort Erie's shoreline also produces steelhead during much of the colder times of the year. Drifters work a Kwikfish near the bottom for steelies in the winter, walleye in the spring and bass in summer. Winter anglers also use egg sacks when drifting, while shore casters send out big minnows.

The most consistent warm-water species in the upper river is the smallmouth bass. When the season opens, boaters and shoreline casters key on these plentiful fish. Bass can be taken from the base of the Peace Bridge downriver to the last navigable areas below Grand Island. Anglers get on the water well before sunrise early in the summer and cast to the rocky edges as the boat moves downcurrent. Jigs, crankbaits, and heavy spinners all take bass, but time of day is more important here. River traffic gets heavy by mid-morning and boat control becomes difficult.

Every accessible breakwater, pier and dock area along the upper river draws groups of panfishermen. Broderick Park at the foot of Ferry Street is the scene of many a bucket-filling session when the yellow and white perch move close to shore. Live minnows or white Twister-tailed jigs do well along the edge of the river's current.

Winter sees a modest number of ice fishermen drilling holes— mainly for smelt and perch—around Beaver Island State Park on Grand Island, the bays north of Fort Erie, and the horseshoe bay formed by Strawberry Island (accessible only by boat).

Any time you fish the Head Of The River or the upper Niagara River, you can plan on powerful currents worthy of respect. Fortunately, those very same currents are also a powerful attractor for a wide range of hard fighting game fish worth doing battle with.

Chapter 14

Adrift

Sport fishing pioneers crossed Lake Erie in vessels not much larger than uncovered wagons. At the start of the Twentieth Century, privately owned boats began appearing along the shoreline at dockage or pulled up on beaches. The leisure-boating sales market was far from booming just after the first world war, but signs were visible of a move towards non-commercial fishing. People were beginning to show interest in catching fish by hand, not just with traps and nets.

Names such as Lyman, Thompson, Shell Lake and Cayuga appeared on the sides of small boats somewhere near the stern and "kickers" (small outboard motors) such as the Elto and Martin were putting small parties of fishermen out to deeper waters than could be reached by casting.

Most early outboard motors could not be idled low enough to allow anglers to use the technique we today call trolling. Most trolling was done with a pair of oars, a touch of grease in the oar locks and a fishing pole stuck out of each corner of the transom.

Those simpler days saw slender-shaped boats, heavy silk and dacron lines, assorted June-Bug spinners, large-hooked Yellow Sally flies, brass-wire spreaders and a small outboard motor that took a lot of oil to keep from burning out.

One of the handiest tools of the fish-finding trade before the advent of small, affordable sonar devices was the "soap on a stone" trick used by many fishermen in search of gravel, sand and stone bottoms. Somewhere on board was a bar of soap in a dish of water. To check the bottom the angler would have a stone or perhaps some other flat-bottomed object tied to a rope. If it was a stone he would rub it with soft soap, send it to the bottom, bounce it once or twice and then bring it back to the surface.

With knots on the line to mark depths, fishermen could read approximate water depths. The soft soap would bring up samples of the type of bottom over which they were fishing; or at least, scratches in the soap might show what was down there. Today, of course, any good graph-type sonar unit gives those readings at a glance. On the other hand, the old time rock-and-rope system didn't need wiring or costly insurance.

Most of these techniques would still find fish today, but the modern angler would just as soon let the electronics tell him the depth, type of bottom, and water conditions. Then he can start fishing while the screen shows him all the fish he hasn't caught yet.

Drifting: The Long and Short of It

Drift-fishing has played an important part in the fishing done on Lake Erie through the years. It remains so to this day.

Many anglers find a stretch of water with walleye-holding structures, and work it simply by drifting downwind and trolling back over that structure into the wind. Tony Orsini caught the prize walleye described in the introduction by trolling into the wind in the same way he had trolled as a kid decades earlier on Lake Erie. He admits that he wasn't quite sure whether he was trolling or stillfishing, but the results were still well worth reporting.

Troll up and drift down is probably a technique as old as the use of small boats for sport fishing. "Up" means against the wind, of course, while "down" means with the wind. In days when outboard motors could not be used to troll effectively, most anglers would settle for a good drifting wind and travel several miles before returning to the start of their drift or home port.

Since conventional wisdom had it that walleye were bottom-holding fish like their cousin the yellow perch, most walleye drifters stuck with the three-way rig: a double leader with a heavy weight on one line and a longer leader with a spinner and worm on the other. The spinner was usually a June Bug with a nightcrawler threaded on a Yellow Sally fly. Thousands of walleye and possibly millions of blue pike were taken this way from the bottom structures of Lake Erie between World War I and World War II. The fish were abundant then, and any drift would eventually take the boat over a cooperative school of fish. Many fishermen of that era were able to sell the excesses of their success, which was legal back then, to fish houses or area restaurants.

After the introduction of smooth-running trolling motors, both gas and later electric, drift fishing receded somewhat into the background, but it remained a favorite technique with many boaters on Lake Erie.

Commercial fishermen were first to discover that walleye did not always hold near the bottom. Drifting along with a lure or baited hook set at a suspended depth, it was found, could sometimes result in more walleye than the lines set close to the bottom.

A Suspense Story

Capt. Bob Jaycox Sr. relates how he accidentally discovered the fact that schools of walleye suspend heavily in Lake Erie. Before the banning of commercial fishing with gill nets, Jaycox had been a highly successful commercial fishermen netting out of Lorain Harbor. Like everyone else, by the early 1950's he was no longer getting many blue pike and had to concentrate on yellow perch—a fish which relates to bottom contours.

As commercial fishing for perch increased, fewer and fewer nets were set at depths anywhere but on the bottom. One afternoon in the summer of 1955, Jaycox was at the wheel of his fish tug as hands were setting out nets off the transom. He told a hand to go back and throw out another "box", meaning let out another length of netting contained in one box.

Instead, the hand threw out the connected box and none on board noticed the box and floating section of net. When they returned the next day and began picking fish out of the net, the crew discovered that as they approached the near-surface section of netting, they found more and more big walleyes. They picked up the floating box and continued picking progressively fewer walleye as the net settled down to the bottom depths at which it was intentionally set. Clearly, walleyes were moving at depths somewhere near the surface.

Commercial fishermen on Lake Erie had use of the then expensive Bendix Depth Recorder shortly after World War II, and many chart readers were probably aware that massive schools of fish much larger than bait were appearing on the screen well above the bottom. But it wasn't until the blue pike disappeared that commercial fishermen had to start looking for alternative fish to harvest from the lake.

Several years later, sport fishermen began drift fishing over these suspended schools of walleye in the Western Basin of Lake Erie and the rest is sport fishing history.

Good drift fishermen plan their outing well before the day of the trip, by watching weather forecasts. Drifts depend on the direction and intensity of winds; a slight change in wind direction can throw off an entire presentation.

Walleye schools, in particular, will key in on a heavy bait school and follow it well away from the temperatures and clarity conditions the books say are typical for walleye. Lure color combinations become critical when water clarity and unusual wave action alter the patterns of fish movement. Hence, it is not unusual to board a drift boat in the Western Basin and see a wire or rack strung with a hundred or more weight and color combinations of weight-forward spinners. Erie Dearie, Hot'N Tot's Pygmy, Nite Crawler and others add vivid color to dashboards and gunwales of many a boat that drifts waters in the Western Basin.

Drifting Deep Down
Drifting with bottom bumping spinner-and-worm rigs calls for the

same advanced technology as planer boarding and downrigging, namely on-board sonar equipment. As for the lures themselves, there is much variance as to size, color, length, etc. Expert drifters keep a selection of tied rigs in much the same way that trout fishermen keep collections of flies.

A color selector device is as necessary in deep-water drifting as it is in trolling suspended levels over deeper water. Fish can turn on and off with subtle changes in light penetration and/or wind direction. When light patterns shift, alternative finishes need to be tried. Silver in bright sunlight might suddenly be replaced by a gold-hammered finish when clouds move through and skies darken. Another less observable change is the clarity from one area to another. Even when surface waters appear to remain the same, changes of clarity near the bottom can slow or stop fish responses. Walleye are said to have cones in their eyes which have a high receptivity to the color orange, but ask Ted Malota of Wanakah and the dominant color would be chartreuse green. Malota keeps single- and double-bladed chartreuse spinner blades in good numbers. The addition of beads in red, green, or yellow can sometimes increase fish strikes even more effectively than changing to a different shape of spinner blade.

Wave action influences deep-water drifting presentations. "Old rollers" with a gentle backup breeze combine to make what some call good drifting days. Many fishermen look at these conditions as ideal for drifting bottom rigs.

Along with the spinner-and-worm, other lures have a place in deep drifting. The banana-type lures (Kwikfish, Flatfish, Lazy Ike, etc.) all have a built-in action that does well in deep water. The lift and drop of wave action tends to make these lures work with an erratic action that triggers strikes. These lures can be doctored so that the tail hook can be fixed with a nightcrawler and still retain some of that side-to-side motion. Most banana-type lures only need the tail hook to track properly and an oversized treble on the tail makes hooking a nightcrawler a simpler task.

While many Erie anglers are locked on a trolling course for the duration of the summer, some anglers have rediscovered drifting—at both suspended and bottom depths—and come in with lunker-sized walleyes, bass and perch during the entire warm-weather boating season. Drifting has a storied past here, and today, many successful Lake Erie boaters, using sophisticated sonar and Loran readings, locate and drift over fish-holding structures everywhere from Toledo to Buffalo.

Drift-fishing is much more than a pleasant memory on Lake Erie.

RON KEIL / OHIO DNR

Chapter 15

The Rise in Fall Perch

As cooling breezes arrive each morning and the leaves in the trees start to change, most sportsmen begin to think and talk of hunting. For many of Lake Erie's regular fishermen, however, the quarry is neither furred nor feathered—it's striped, and it's pleasantly available during those marvelous days of autumn.

Every fall perch fishing season arrives differently. Some years, the fish begin schooling in the deeper waters of the Central and Eastern Basins—usually at 60 to 70-foot depths—well before the arrival of Labor Day. Perch hunters follow these schools into progressively shallower water as the fall season progresses. Conversely, perch may remain scattered or refuse to feed heavily until the first frost. Usually, a late season, with open and accessible water in November and December, results in a few exceptional days of perch fishing. Best days occur whenever a warm front moves through.

However the fall perch season unfolds, a few principles will hold. Regardless of prevailing signs, favorable or poor, perch will eventually begin schooling sometime before the formation of ice. Also,

while most perch anglers keep records of good fish-holding structures, it is also important to find channels along which fish will travel during their seasonal migrations.

Loran readings, sometimes called "waypoints," can be entered into the unit to mark the hot spots where perch have been caught in days and seasons past. But migrational patterns become easier to follow when the angler has a good handle on the direction (usually shoreward) of the perch schools. Again, good topographical maps will indicate these channels or perch lanes from the deeps to the shallower structures. Following these movements is not complicated, but the hunt involves steady pursuit. Most experts at following these perch movements have become expert by being on the water several times a week. If such lavish amounts of free time don't befall you, your best recourse is regular consultation with the local bait and tackle shop owner. These guys generally receive copious amounts of feedback from perch-hunting customers.

It's very important to remember that the yellow perch is basically a bottom-relating creature. On rare occasion, a school of perch may briefly leave the bottom to chase a bait school, but the percentages heavily favor your finding these fish within two or three feet of bottom whether that bottom be rocks, gravel, sand or mud. By the way, bottom rigs so designed as to allow multiple bait offerings are standard equipment for Lake Erie perch.

Another notable feature of perch is their adherence to a daytime feeding schedule. Perch feed almost exclusively by sight, or at least so it is believed. It is rare, indeed, to hit perch after sunset, and predawn outings are equally futile. Things rarely start to happen until sunlight begins to penetrate the deeper waters. Anglers who find themselves out on the water during hours of darkness are best advised to seek out bass, walleye or muskellunge.

Light Touches in the Deeps

More often than not, good catches of perch are the result of good rod readings—knowing when to respond to light taps on the line. Unless the perch are feeding heavily, most hits will be gentle tugs or "hang bites," in Erie parlance.

First, there is the factor of line length and stretching. When you're 60-70 feet down, line stretch can be considerable. Serious perch anglers invest in quality monofilament line with little stretch. The slight extra cost of line is far outweighed by the great increase in perch hooked and boated.

Rod tip action also makes a difference. Many serious anglers buy custom rods for the bigger game fish they pursue, but give little thought to their panfishing equipment. Yet a good "perch rod" often increases the percentages of fish hooked and brought to bucket. Length isn't as important as tip action and taper. The rod with a relatively light tip, fast action and medium butt section is ideal. This rod design is available in baitcasting and spinning rods from five- to eight-foot lengths. What length to buy is more a matter of handling and storage than anything.

Most perchers use some sort of spreader device to increase their hits and catches. The classic brass-wire spreader with its sliding weight still sees many hours of use on perch both from a boat and through the ice. Today, the fine-wire spreader has begun to catch on with perch fishermen for many reasons. First, the fine wires allow anglers to detect the slightest of hits. Also, the new spreader models allow for switching weights so that weight can be reduced on calm days or when fishing shallow; heavier weights can be snapped on when in deeper water or when fishing in high, rolling waves. One additional feature of the newer spreaders is that they are designed with a variety of spinner blades and beads of various colors.

Color and the Perch

Anyone who follows VHF fish talk on Lake Erie for any length of time quickly learns that there is a continuous dialogue regarding what lure finishes are currently catching the fish. As the sun rises overhead and later settles toward the horizon, effective color combinations can change, sometimes several times in the course of the day.

Multiple rods with spreaders allow for the simultaneous presentation of a wide variety of colors and metallic finishes. In addition, many experts affix colored beads and blades on the monofilament leader just above the hook. Let's say you have a spreader rigged with a chartreuse blade on one hook and a plain hook on the other. You may find that most or even all the fish you catch will have hit either one or the other.

Any good system of spreader colors should include the following finishes: chrome, brass, copper, chartreuse, yellow, green, red and orange. Look to these same colors when choosing your "flickers"— the little beads and blades described elsewhere in this book.

Minnow Power

Triton, the Classical Greek sea god, had mythical power over minnows, but minnows are themselves powerful bait for those who anchor in Lake Erie waters for perch. Grubs, nightcrawlers, leeches, and other live bait offerings will catch a few perch from time to time, but for consistent catches of big perch in Lake Erie, it's a bucket full of minnows every time.

Inland lake fishermen sometimes question the hook sizes offered in tackle stores along the Erie shoreline. Rather than the size eight or six hooks usually recommended for perch, here you'll see cards of size four and even size two prominently displayed. Also, the minnows sold for perch bait around these parts often look like they're better suited for bass or walleye fishing.

The size of the minnow sold in local bait shops will vary somewhat depending on availability, but the regulars look for minnows bigger than those associated with crappie fishing. Emerald shiners, sometimes called "buckeyes," grow steadily through the summer season, resulting in few "leftovers" during the spring perch run but many big baits during the fall run. Quite often, bait dealers are accused of trying to dip out the big ones for customers when, in fact, this size bait is the right bait for perch in Lake Erie. That these baits can work becomes abundantly clear when perch are brought up from any great depth and minnows (not the one on the hook) pop out of their mouths. These regurgitated specimens may be even larger than the minnows that are being used on the hook.

Chapter 16

When Winter Comes

Ice fishing on Lake Erie has both a storied past and a bright future, its popularity growing yearly. Before the practice was banned by law, fishermen were once seen crossing the ice with sleds drawn by dogs. Later, old cars were stripped of excess metal and loaded with fishing gear. Many times, the "ice jalopy" traffic along the lake was heavier than adjacent street traffic along the shoreline.

Modern day ice fishermen now run several miles from shore with the use of snowmobiles, four-wheel trucks and other types of off-road vehicles suitable for winter use.

It's fun. It's an inexpensive way to catch fish. It's relaxing. It's rewarding. And it requires caution—at all times.

Most ice fishing catch reports involve yellow perch and walleye, and each year the bulk of those reports come from two areas which comprise less than 10 percent of the lake's surface. In fact, only a part of the main body of the lake is fully ice-covered in most winters. In general, safe ice will occur primarily at the extreme western end of the Western Basin and the extreme eastern end of the Eastern Basin.

With the city of Buffalo in the background, a N.Y. Power Authority chopper checks out the current ice conditions. The reports it files will be of use to ice fishermen here. Photo by N.Y. Power Authority.

The Erie County Sheriff's Department, in the Eastern Basin, sends out a helicopter flight each day that the lake is ice-covered. The program, nicknamed "Sundowner Patrol," covers the entire Erie County part of the lake where there's ice, and has been credited with several life-saving rescues. Capt. Kevin Caffery, principal pilot for these patrols, cites miscalculation and poor planning as the cause for nearly all situations where fishermen were stranded and required rescue.

Safety Essentials

In cooperation with the Erie County Sheriff's Department, the Erie County Federation of Sportsmens Clubs has put together a descriptive list of "Safety Necessities" in a pocket-sized folder. This folder includes a map indicating prominent shore markers, locations of landings and other shore features, and basic topographical and compass readings. Here are the six major safety points in the Lake Erie Ice Fishing Safety Advisory list of necessities:

COMPASS. Own and become familiar with using one. Orient

yourself before leaving the shoreline. Know where you are before you go out on the ice. A compass may be needed to get back in case of fog, blowing snow, snowfall, heavy rains or darkness.

FLOATING ICE PICKS. Used to pull yourself out of the water and onto the ice if you should break through. They are easily made with 20-penny nails, heads sawed off, driven into 1 1/2 inch X 6 inch hardwood dowels with the nails protruding one to 1 1/4 inches. Two such picks are connected together with about four feet of strong, light cord and worn hanging around the neck.

FLARES. Used day or night to signal your location if an emergency should arise. Inexpensive railroad flares work fine as do the marine flares most summertime boaters already own.

BLAZE ORANGE. The most highly visible color on the ice. Could be essential if you need to be seen and located for ice warnings or rescue. Inexpensive hunters' vests work very well.

WEATHER FORECASTS & ICE CONDITIONS. Check for impending storms and for wind direction. Stay off the ice during offshore winds. Northeast, East, and Southeast winds are especially dangerous as they cause ice floes to break away from shore. Stay off the ice when it's less than four inches thick, regardless of wind direction.

WHEN & WHERE. Notify someone where you intend to fish and when you expect to return. In case of emergency, this will insure prompt search and rescue efforts.

Additional suggestions include:

1. Extra clothing: gloves, coat, ski mask.

2. Heat Source: heat pack, portable heaters, sterno, hand warmers, matches and lighter.

3. Ice Creepers for ease of walking and jumping over cracks in the ice.

4. 30-40 feet of rope to throw to someone in need.

5. Awareness of the time of any helicopter or airplane safety patrols over your fishing area.

6. Fish with another person whenever possible in case of an accident or injury.

Despite the space these items require, most ice fishermen are able to fit them all into either a backpack or small sled with enough room left over for tackle items.

Bays, Channels & Harbors

A different kind of spirit seems to hold forth among those ice fishermen who stick to the bays, channels and inner harbors of Erie. Unlike their more serious brethren who venture miles out onto the ice and fish over deeper waters, those who gather in protected, nearshore sites seem to have a more relaxed feeling about their fishing. This is not to say that they are indifferent about what they are doing. It's just that they are a friendly lot, and prone to lengthy conversations about whatever aspects of fishing or hunting move them at the moment.

Many reasons can be given for the popularity of this nearshore bay ice fishing: (1) It serves as a sportsman's bridge between the end of deer season and formation of widespread solid ice; (2) Catches are generally better at the beginning of the ice season; (3) It's a great way to introduce young kids to the sport of fishing; (4) There's little effort in getting to the fish, as a short walk is all that's usually necessary; (5) Sites are close enough so that anglers can sometimes get in an hour to two before or after work; and (6) Many people just like to fish relatively close to shore, where the ice is usually safer.

There are several basic considerations in this kind of fishing. A short (24 to 30-inch) ultralight rod with matching small reel is ideal for jigging. String it with fine line such as four-pound test. Selection of line color depends entirely on water coloration in the area fished, but the main choices are blue, green or clear. Effective ice lures can be anything that flutters when the rod tip is dropped. These lures can be small Swedish Pimples, flutter spoons and mini jigs fixed with a fine-wire single hook. Minnows work well, but small bugs last much longer on the hook: mousies, spikes and those grubs found inside of goldenrod stems.

The late Dave Ellis of Derby, New York, developed a real feel for when a panfish had the hook in its mouth. His specialty was putting goodly numbers of big yellow perch on ice. A casual glance at Ellis as he worked a hole would suggest that he was shivering from the cold. In fact, his jigging style consisted of long intervals of continuous jigging a few inches above the bottom. The jigging movement was no more than the three- to five-inch swings of an ultralight rod tip—just to the point where the rod would start to whip. The hit would usually come just after one of these lengthy fluttering sessions. Bigger perch would simply swim over and inhale the bait and lure. Ellis almost always outfished everyone around, and a big part of his secret was simply to pay constant attention to the rod tip when it was at rest. He knew that sometimes the slightest "hang" or appearance of slack is enough to tell you to set the hook into a rod-arching, thick-bodied perch.

Eastern Basin Ice: Places and Techniques

The Eastern Basin ice fishery is confined mostly to the Erie County shoreline of New York State and the Welland Canal to Fort Erie shoreline in Canadian waters. Area ice conditions are reported by the New York State Power Authority, which maintains an "Ice Boom," a chain-linked span of wooden sections strung together across the head of the Niagara River to slow the flow of ice into it. The Erie County Sheriff's Department ice patrol, mentioned earlier, is another source of reports on ice conditions. In addition, warnings are issued at the major accesses, for example the Sturgeon Point access site, when the ice is unsafe.

Public access to ice fishing in the Eastern Basin is mainly from two locations: the Pinehurst access, with limited parking and a steep bluff to climb between the Old Lake Shore Road and the lake; and Sturgeon Point Marina, with ample parking and ease of access to the ice. Anglers running RV's (snowmobiles, trikes, quads, etc.) leave Sturgeon and sometimes travel more than ten miles to find yellow perch and walleye schools.

While walleye can be found and caught off Sturgeon and Pinehurst, the greater number of fishermen concentrate on yellow perch. The rigs ice anglers use for Lake Erie perch, however, are not what most anglers would associate with panfishing. Spreaders are fixed with size #2 hooks and held on sturdy tip-ups. Lake Erie perch tip-ups are often mistaken for ones used to catch walleye and northern pike.

Vertical ice jigging for perch in Erie's deeper waters was once the exclusive technique of a handful of winter fishermen. Now, legions of anglers have caught on to this exciting style of fishing through the many presentations of experts like Dave Bianchi, past president of the

New York Walleye Association. Bianchi has designed a series of lead-head jigs (called "Blockbusters") and has shown prospective ice anglers—sometimes hundreds at a time—how to vary the lifts and drops of the lure so that it entices fish that hold close to the bottom on a frozen lake.

Ice-jigging lure designs are diverse. One of the most universally known is the jigging Rapala. Many experts fish with just this lure in various colors and sizes. Bait may or may not be added to the belly hook. Another walleye jig of note is the Swedish Pimple. This heavy vertical jig does not "swim" in a circle the way a properly presented jigging Rapala will, but it offers a lively action that is sometimes enhanced by the addition of a minnow or strip of minnow. Some anglers will even use chub-sized minnows on the Pimple to entice a walleye. Heddon Sonars and Silver Buddies represent yet another lure design. These stand-up flutter spoons have lead-weighted "bellies" which create a vertical rather than lateral flutter when lifted and dropped. These lures can draw passing fish into a location at times when fish don't seem to be hitting. Even when they aren't taking all the fish, the Sonars and Buddies let you know if there are fish down there.

The most unusual lure design for deep water jigging on Lake Erie ice has to be the Jig-A-Wopper. This lure swims, sinks, flutters and turns with the slightest change of the rod tip. Recent outings on Lake Erie ice have proven the Jig-A-Wopper to be equally effective on perch and walleye. In deeper waters, shades of green, yellow and chartreuse bring up many a perch that tip the scales past the one-pound mark.

Eastern Basin ice requires caution and a long walk or ride most times. But the jumbo perch, good-sized walleye and the occasional lake trout make it all worthwhile.

Western Basin Ice: Places and Techniques
Western Basin ice is not always easy to deal with. Bays and other areas protected by land masses will safely freeze for a while and then a strong wind moves the ice and breaks up what was a winter-long ice field.

Hut operators in this basin began offering guided trip packages in the mid-1980's. There are now a half-dozen major ice fishing guide services in Ottawa County. Any of these guides can give you a first-hand report on ice conditions and the possibilities for fishing access and success. Write or call the Ottawa County Visitors Bureau, 127 W. Perry Street, Port Clinton, Ohio 43452.

When safe ice covers Western Basin waters, unusually large wall-eye (generally bigger than those caught during the summer months) come in during much of the season. Perch fishing, too, gets busy about the same time and often in the same places. Whether planning a trip with one of the many hut operators or putting it together on your own, gear fit for both perch and walleye should be packed and ready to use.

First-ice jiggers go with a different rig in each hand and work both rods with differing lifts until a good perch or walleye pattern can be determined. A minnow-tipped Swedish Pimple on one rod can be balanced out with a fluttering Heddon Sonar or Silver Buddy on the other rod. A smaller jigging Rapala (#3 or #5) lets you know if the perch schools are moving through ice areas which, all too often, were producing only walleyes the year before.

Fishing inside a hut is comfortable and most hut sites produce good fishing. Smart ice jiggers, though, dress warmly enough so that they can get out and explore.

Western Basin walleye hit most often during those peak periods of early morning and early evening—the change-of-light times at which bait is disoriented and easier prey.

Upbeat catches are often the result of persistent hole hopping. A good day might result in 30-40 holes drilled and much valuable fishing information gathered. True, this approach to ice fishing can be exhausting—few anglers need a sleeping pill after this kind of a day on the ice—but the insights are worth the effort. The person who jigs and digs gets a jump on what's happening (size and species) and he goes back the next day or time with much of the ground work already laid.

Part Three

Tributary Tributes

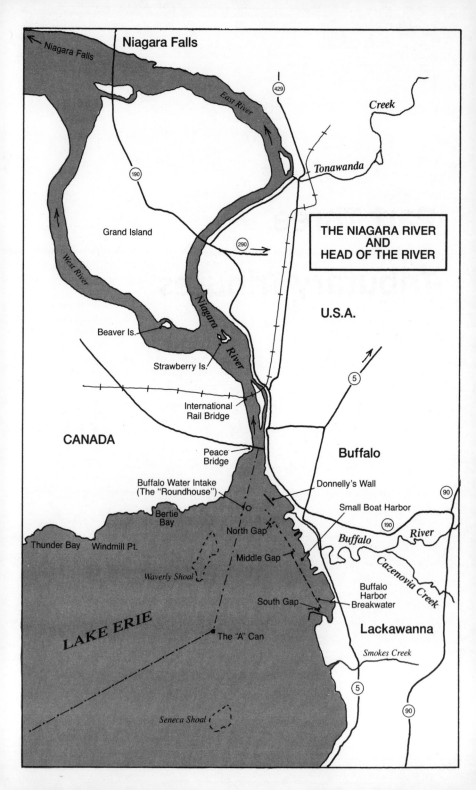

Chapter 17

The Menu

The lower sections of many Lake Erie tributaries are greater in size than many prominent inland lakes. Placed in the middle of New York State, for example, the Detroit, the Maumee, the Sandusky and the Niagara (Erie's outlet) would all rank as mid-sized bodies of water among the six largest Finger Lakes.

On the other hand, there are tributaries, or sections of tributaries, where quiet intimacy is the rule. For the contemplative angler who measures success in terms of solitude and quality of experience, Lake Erie tributaries can also accommodate.

The glorious comeback of Erie has, happily, worked its way up into the web of large and small feeders. Once nearly as polluted as the lake itself—indeed, often the very conveyors of that pollution—the tribs are now cleaner, brighter, more inviting. On the big ones, boats are heading out with high hopes and returning with well-stocked fish boxes. And on the smaller ones, both bank and wader fishermen are cashing in.

All this is not to say that Erie tributary fishing is on a par with that of the other Great Lakes. It isn't. If you come here expecting to find what you might have experienced on Lake Ontario's Salmon River, for example, you will for the most part be disappointed. The massive runs of Pacific salmon that thrill anglers on that great river, and other prominent Great Lakes feeders, do not occur here. The runs are both smaller and more brief and, if anything, management is moving away from king and coho salmon. Neither does the steelheading match what you'll find on the Salmon of New York, the Brule of Wisconsin, or a whole host of other legendary Great Lakes tribs. Still, both the salmon and the trout do mount runs into Erie tributaries, and steelhead fishing in particular may build in the years ahead. In addition, both warm water game fish and panfish from the lake ascend certain tribs at times.

Many Lake Erie tributaries wend their way very far inland. In this book, though, we will look at these rivers only as far inland as the first barrier impassable by fish. The greater part of the discussion will center on lake-run fish. Resident stream fish of many kinds can also be encountered of course.

In this chapter, we will provide some background data on Lake Erie tributaries as a whole. This should provide a springboard from which to launch your own piscatorial attack on any Erie trib. In the next chapter, we'll discuss the larger or better tributaries one by one. Keep in mind, though, that even the smaller tribs can at times offer up excitement. The Vermilion River, the Huron River, the Portage River—While not given a great deal of space in this book, these and many other small to mid-sized feeders can, at times, come to life. Finally, in Chapter 19, we will go over in considerable detail some fishing techniques that have proven themselves on Erie's contributory waters.

The Lake-Run Salmonids

Lake Erie tributaries see runs of five imported salmonids: steelhead trout, rainbow trout, brown trout, chinook salmon and coho salmon. Easily, the one most discussed, sought and hooked is the steelhead. Successful spawning of all these fish in the Erie tributaries is very minimal. The fishing is made possible through vigorous stocking programs.

Much attention is given to the jumbo chinook salmon that are caught by boaters in the open water of the lake. The impressive sizes these fish attain make them attractive trophy prospects. But for day-to-day stream fishing along the banks of Lake Erie feeder streams, the steelhead has become king. King salmon are mainly stocked in New York streams and appear only infrequently in feeder streams along the Central and Western Basins of the lake.

Rainbow trout are considerably different from steelhead trout in their movements in both lakes and streams. Floyd Cornelius, Senior Aquatic Biologist in charge of cold-water studies at the Lake Erie Fisheries Unit in Dunkirk, offers the following distinction between rainbow and steelhead trout: "Rainbows do not move around the lake nor do they imprint to their stocking site. Steelhead undergo smoltification (in natural conditions they go from fresh to salt water), imprint to their natal stream and migrate long distances during their open-lake stage."

Brown trout are a bonus. Experienced trout and salmon anglers have the least success at predicting, among all the salmonids, the upstream runs of browns. Generally, browns enter the tributaries sometime after the first runs of steelhead and rainbow trout, which often means early November. After this period, all forecasts are off. Experts speculate that browns, being the voracious feeders that they are, follow available bait schools. If bait fish move up into a particular stream, or section of stream, brown trout may too and they will continue to be caught until the bait scatters or leaves.

Coho salmon are somewhat more predictable in their stream runs but the future stocking of this fish is in question. Cohos appear in streams between mid-October and mid-November, though some will come a month early and some will stay a month later. They will not hold in either small or large streams throughout the winter, as will the steelhead. A good yardstick for the coho run would be "first frost till first freeze." One notable exception is where warm water outlets enter. The power plant in Dunkirk Harbor, for example, might hold a coho school all winter long. Unfortunately, shorebound casters have limited access to this area.

Recently, New York State officials have been reconsidering stocking policies on cohos, mainly because angler preferences and catch reports seem to skew to other species—principally steelhead. However, at this writing, the state's DEC has not made public its intentions regarding the stocking of this, the smaller of the two "Pacific" salmon.

Another salmonid that has been tentatively introduced to Lake Erie tributary waters is the skamania strain of steelhead trout. This strain shows a much greater tolerance to warm waters and may hold in shallow waters—including streams and rivers—for up to five months of the year. Bacterial kidney disease caused the cancellation of the 1989 stocking of this heat-tolerant rainbow, but indications are that the skamania could have a promising future in Lake Erie's tributaries. The few skamania that have been caught have been at or below the five pound mark, but some may eventually grow to 10 pounds and beyond.

Skamania behavior in Lake Erie is most unusual, according to William Culligan, Unit Leader of the Lake Erie Unit at Dunkirk, New York. Culligan comments that these heat-tolerant salmonids retain those instinctive spawning patterns developed while running up the long rivers and streams of the Pacific northwest—mainly in Washington state. They spawn in January and February, but most angler contact in New York waters can be expected in the months of September, October and November, depending greatly on height of stream flow. When stream levels are high, Culligan notes, winter anglers may encounter these fish for periods longer than five months. In any event, the exact timing of a skamania run is difficult to predict. In a season with high water levels, skamania may show in the streams as early as August; seasons with low water levels may not see a skamania run until well into November.

Tributary fishing cannot match the level of intensity seen in Lakes Michigan and Ontario. King salmon, the biggest and heaviest of the salmonids, rarely exceed 20 pounds when caught in either Lake Erie or any of its feeder streams. There is little emphasis on producing big salmonids in Lake Erie's waters.

Fishery stocking agencies in Ohio, Pennsylvania and New York have drastically cut back or eliminated the stocking of kings. Ohio discontinued the stocking of kings in 1979. Pennsylvania's king salmon stocking numbers went from 748,340 (1985) to 63,100 (1986) to 52,000 (1987). None have been stocked since 1988.

Only New York State continues to stock king salmon, and the entire effort (approximately 500,000 fish) is in Cattaraugus Creek, with possible surplus fish introduced in Eighteen Mile Creek from Lake Ontario excesses.

It is entirely possible for king salmon to make runs up Ohio and Pennsylvania streams, even though they are only stocked in New York tribs. The Grand River shallows, above Painesville, sees a modest run of kings each fall in the midst of its steelhead run. The higher the water, the greater the salmon run. Again, though, the biggest salmon rarely exceed twenty pounds. Most of the big Grand River kings are more slender than Lake Ontario kings of the same age. Anything over 15 pounds in these waters is trophy status.

Steelhead trout in Lake Erie tributaries more closely match the size of steelies in Lakes Michigan and Ontario. Stream-running fish generally fall in the 2- to 6-pound range, but 10-pound-plus fish appear more frequently each year.

Steelhead stocking figures vary for the Eastern and Central basin areas, but the combined total stocking is generally between 1.5 and two million fish. Combine these with the skamania additions from Pennsylvania and the rainbow trout plantings of approximately 75,000 fish in New York and Pennsylvania, and you can see that there is plenty for Erie stream fishermen to get excited about.

Brown trout stocking totals less than 200,000 fish, but some of these spring and fall fingerlings eventually attain weights of 15 pounds. It is not uncommon for a wading angler to be seen running upstream with a whining drag on his reel only to find that the king salmon he thought he had hooked was a brown trout somewhere in the double-figure category. Brown trout feed well in the open waters of Lake Erie, principally on smelt and alewives, and when they do ascend the feeder streams they have great girth, weight and fighting ability. On average, however, most browns fall in the 2- to 6-pound range—similar to the size of the steelies encountered here.

Yet another salmonid recently introduced to Lake Erie tributaries is the seeforellen strain of brown trout. Theories are that this scrappy, fast-growing European version of *Salmo trutta* could possibly attain a weight of 40 pounds in Lake Erie waters. At even half that size, seeforellen browns would rank with king salmon as the largest salmonids entering the feeder streams of Lake Erie.

Noteworthy resident populations of warm water fish do not exist in Eastern Basin trib waters, according to warm-water fisheries specialist Don Einhouse. Most come up from the lake. The most dominant species to enter Eastern Basin feeder streams each spring is the smallmouth bass. However, Einhouse states that many of these fish are entering for purposes of spawning—generally when the temperatures reach 60 degrees—and do not remain upstream for a prolonged period after spawning. All too often, these fish leave the streams before the legal opening of the bass fishing season in New York State, which is the third Saturday in June.

The Western Basin, on the other hand, offers good warm-water fishing in and well above the mouths of most major streams. The various species of fish which enter and predominate feeder streams in Ohio's western waterways—walleye, smallmouth bass, white bass, yellow perch and white perch—will be discussed in detail in Chapter 18.

When to Go

Peak seasons for most salmonids in the tributaries are spring and fall, with the fall run drawing a slight edge. Fish movements in the fall are more predictable and current flow is generally more stable. Melting ice and snow in the high mountains above feeder streams may leave these waters roiled and muddy for several days in the spring. Fall runoffs are not as lengthy and allow stream fishermen more time to get in on the action.

Spring tributary fishing arrives at different times each season. The mountains of New York, Pennsylvania and eastern Ohio send down heavy runoffs as ice and snow cover melt. Each day calls for a careful watch of air temperatures. On a typical early spring morning, first light will bring cool, nighttime waters followed by a temperature rise at mid-morning. By noon, however, those same waters may be recooled by melted ice and snow. The sunny, midday stream may actually be colder and less likely to produce pronounced fish movement and feeding. Also, midday might see your chosen river turbid and silt-laden, again as a result of snow melt brought on by the higher sun.

Peak periods for the warm-water species (bass, walleye, panfish, etc.) in the tributaries is late spring and early summer. Weather conditions dictate when these fish enter bays and feeder streams. While some species follow seasonal patterns, no timetable can be set on stream-run bass. Like brown trout, bass chase whatever bait schools are moving, wherever they are moving. Lake-run emerald shiners or "buckeyes" are one bait fish the bass are liable to pursue.

The peak activity takes place near the stream mouths, and lasts only as long as the bait fish are there. Like the overlooked bass fishery which exists in the open waters of Lake Erie, the tributary bass run had until recently gone virtually unnoticed. Yet it is one of the simplest and most comfortable ways of introducing young anglers to the sport of fishing. Walking a stream bank for bass can be full of action at the right time and place.

One tip worth noting when fishing all streams of any size is to continually monitor the water temperature. King salmon, rainbow trout and steelhead generally prefer waters in the lower 50's. Browns don't begin showing up until the temperatures rise to the high 50's, and skamania steelhead may appear once waters reach the lower 60's. A simple, hand-held thermometer is handy, because stream waters can change quickly. Here, shore-bound anglers have an advantage. When conditions are adverse, they can simply move up or downstream— or to another stream—where factors are more favorable.

Another consideration is water level. Warm or low water along the lake shoreline will, for example, cause a late upstream fall run in the Rocky River in Western Ohio and Chautauqua Creek in Western New York. All rivers have their own patterns but generally, low water in early fall signals a late run. A late run in both small and large streams will also mean more fish taken with spawn and fewer fish taken with artificials (spinners and spoons) once the run does get under way.

Chapter 18

The Rivers

This chapter will focus on some of the major tributaries. This should not prompt you to ignore the smaller feeder streams, which can draw tremendous runs of game fish at times.

Moving from east to west, here are summaries of ten of Erie's largest and/or most important tributaries.

New York

EIGHTEEN MILE CREEK. This is the first public-accessible and wadable stream west of Buffalo. This impressive creek, located on the Hamburg/Evans town line, splits into east and west branches above Route 20, and affords the wading angler excellent opportunities. To gain access to the best fishing sites at the mouth, you must walk some distance downstream from either the Old Lake Shore Road or the Route 5 bridge.

Together, the two branches offer stream-walking anglers a total of more than 30 miles of stream in a wild looking setting. Upstream, it winds through fields and wood lots, while in its lower stretches it cuts through steep cliffs as it approaches the lake's shore.

Shorecasting at the mouth of Eighteen Mile Creek can be very productive at times. Waders and bank fishermen cast for trout and salmon in the early spring and mid-fall. The same shoreline positions will produce walleye and smallmouth bass during the morning and evening hours of the late spring and early summer season.

Fifty thousand fall fingerling coho and 25,000 spring yearling steelhead are stocked in the two branches of Eighteen Mile Creek. When available, surplus chinook salmon are also placed in these waters.

Although not stocked in this creek, brown trout follow the runs of other salmonids in both spring and fall.

Angling specialists like Dick Bennett of Eden look at this stream as a good yardstick of the recovery and restoration of tributary fishing here. Bennett will cover several miles along both branches with an assortment of artificial and natural baits. His approaches include a study of the solunar tables for peak fishing periods, a thermometer to check on water temperatures, a lure "color selector," polarized sunglasses, and a sturdy pair of waders to stay comfortable while in the water. Bennett will catch hundreds of trout and salmon each season (most of which are immediately released), but this former president of the Erie County Chapter of Bassmasters continually stresses in his fishing class presentations that both Eighteen Mile and many other Western New York feeder streams are also havens for smallmouth bass. These bass can be taken with a fly rod or light spinning tackle. Bronzebacks make several post-spawning runs up these feeder streams virtually unnoticed by anglers who are otherwise well informed about stream runs of walleye, trout and salmon. The same Super Vibrax spinners that take big steelies in the fall can draw the attention of smallies during the morning and evening hours of early summer.

Lake Erie boaters have long known of the great smallmouth fishing that occurs in late June and early July along rocky shoreline structures. Recently, stream-mouth fishermen have been catching on to the bass bonanza that occurs just after the New York State season opener (third Saturday in June) in Eighteen Mile and other nearby tribs.

CATTARAUGUS CREEK. This creek is really river-sized. The

lower river (mouth to first impassable barrier) is a wide, meandering flowage nearly 30 miles in length. It begins at the Springville Power Dam and surrenders to the big lake at Irving, one mile north of the Route 5 and 20 Bridge. Accesses to the fishable areas of the Cattaraugus lie mainly along lands of the Seneca Indians. Most anglers obtain New York State and Seneca Nations licenses before fishing the upstream areas. Approximately 12 miles of the nearly 30-mile lower section flow through New York State lands, but access is severely limited.

The deeper waters at the mouth mean that Cattaraugus is also a good destination for small-boat anglers. Here there is good bass fishing in the summer and trout and salmon action in the spring and fall. Boaters usually can troll upstream to the first or second rail bridge without running aground.

Waders can either enter at an access in the lower stretches of Seneca Nations land and work upstream or drive up to Gowanda and work downstream. One interesting approach is to put in a small car-

The end of the line for lake-run fish in Cattaraugus Creek. The power dam at Springville, N. Y. is a gathering point for many shore casters and waders, who come here to try for both trout and salmon.

topper or canoe at the Aldrich Street bridge in Gowanda, float down-stream and fish the larger pools all the way down to the state or private marinas near the mouth of the river.

The late Ben Wojda, marina operator and life-long observer of the river, watched its potential develop. Wojda continually remarked that most people—even local residents—were little aware of the great numbers, sizes and kinds of fish that go in and out of Cattaraugus each season. To date, the creek is still referred to by fishery biologists as one of the best kept fishing secrets in New York State. It is also the largest tributary entering Lake Erie in New York State.

The U.S. Army Corp. of Engineers has done extensive breakwa-ter construction at the mouth of Cattaraugus. Two walls improve access for shoreline fishermen. The west breakwater extends into the lake to water depths of six feet. Typically, casters have better results with the trout and salmon than most boaters in the fall. From mid-September until mid-October, when the fish leave the mouth area and gather upstream, casters eagerly deploy spinners, spoons, egg sacks and—a week or two into the run—skein sections. They fish both from the banks and from the breakwater at the mouth of the creek.

Pennsylvania

WALNUT AND ELK CREEKS. Pennsylvania's two major trib-utaries—both located west of Erie—are similar in size, geography and fish species. Walnut offers approximately 15 miles of fishable stream; Elk offers close to 20 miles. The creeks flow through steep mountainous terrain—typical of the entire Pennsylvania shore-line—and cut escarpments as they enter the lake. Both streams are stocked with the same number of coho, approximately 150,000 year-ly. Neither stream receives steelhead, but steelies make heavy runs each spring and fall from the stocking of approximately 500,000 fish in adjacent Pennsylvania streams.

A put-and-take stocking of brown trout (greater in Elk Creek) brings rows of anglers on opening day each spring. The streams see heavy pressure for the first week, but things settle down a bit after that. Robert Kenyon, fisheries biologist with the Fairview Lake Erie Research Unit, remarks that anglers crowding in for the fall coho run can make things as hectic as during the spring brown trout gathering. Kenyon recommends high water conditions in all seasons on these streams. When the streams rise, coho, steelies and many warm-water species are likely to appear in a few short hours.

The creeks differ in their settings. Walnut Creek borders the City of Erie and flows several miles through Erie's suburbs. Although not as long as Elk Creek, Walnut is much deeper at its mouth. The state-operated Walnut Creek Marina harbors midsized fishing and pleasure craft, with boat traffic confined mainly to the lake itself. The mouth of Elk Creek is wider and shallower, offering good fishing opportunities for stream waders beginning at the beach.

Ohio

CONNEAUT CREEK. This is one of the largest "creeks" feeding into Lake Erie. Meandering west and then east, Conneaut's fishable waters flow through two states: Pennsylvania and Ohio.

The mouth of Conneaut is protected by a semicircular jetty wall which draws passing schools of steelhead as they congregate at the mouth of the creek in spring and fall. Boat fishermen can either fish the harbor or run upstream approximately a half mile to an impassable rail bridge. Ohio's wadable section of the Conneaut continues inland nearly 20 miles, and there is an additional 20 miles of stream in Pennsylvania.

Fall steelhead fishing pressure is in evidence from the lake's shoreline at the mouth upstream to the state line. Shore casters take positions along the beach and the west jetty wall just after ice-out in the spring and after the arrival of the first cooling temperatures of early fall. In the fall, boaters troll shallow-running spinners, spoons and body baits in the deeper waters near the lake. At the same time, shore casters can reach passing steelies with floating egg sacks and weighted casting spoons and spinners.

Above the rail bridge, waders start working the creek above Keefus Road on the west side of Conneaut. Ohio Wildlife fishery personnel suggest a drive upstream to stream waters above the covered bridge at Middle Road. This upper stretch has retained its soothing, bucolic character as it flows through scenic farm country. Only dedicated trout anglers venture this far upstream—mainly fly-casting purists. The walk can be a long one, but the scenery and fishing reward the effort.

ASHTABULA RIVER. Ashtabula is an Indian word meaning "river of many fish." There are fish, lots of them, but commerce and industry are long-established here. Steamboats began using the harbor as early as 1837. Huge lake freighters enter and depart from the harbor the season long. Several marinas line the shoreline, and offer dockage for hundreds of privately owned boats. Many are cruiser-sized and large enough to venture far offshore.

The industrial complex in Ashtabula Harbor may seem forbidding, and certainly no classic backdrop for some quiet angling. In fact, there is no fishing at all for the first two miles up from the lake. Nonetheless, the Ashtabula hosts sundry fish species and there are many fishing spots south of the city, beginning at Indian Trail Park. Boaters and bank fishermen alike, during the summer season, can find excellent smallmouth and a variety of panfish in waters above the restricted area.

Typically, though, the most downstream point where serious angling is done is that point where motor boats can no longer travel. Depending on water levels, this may be somewhat above the Rt. 84 bridge. Upstream, 15 miles of winding stream awaits waders and bank fishermen. Notable steelhead runs are often encountered.

Perhaps the most distinctive feature of the Ashtabula is its remarkable winding curves as it flows north-northwest toward Lake Erie. Even more pronounced than an oxbow or elbow, many of these curves form nearly completes circles, with some of the circles being a mile or more in diameter. These gradual, winding turns create pockets and undercuts which make perfect holding lies for the steelhead which mount runs throughout the fall and much of the winter as well.

Mike Rawson, fisheries biologist with Ohio's Fairport Unit, remarks that improved water quality in Lake Erie and Ashtabula Harbor is contributing to better fishing prospects all around the area: stream and stream mouth included. Once a heavily-polluted commercial harbor, Ashtabula is making a proud comeback.

GRAND RIVER. The name grand is aptly applied to this, the longest and most productive steelhead stream feeding into Lake Erie.

Boaters have access to the Grand at Fairport Harbor and Painesville. The lower Grand provides about three miles of water deep enough to be fished from a boat, but riffles and shallow pools above Painesville abruptly terminate fishing. In those lower miles, boaters either troll or anchor at points along bends in the river. Despite the preponderance of privately owned land along the heavily populated river-mouth section, parking and many public-accessible areas are available to shore anglers. The Lake Metroparks system maintains six parks open to fishing, beginning with Helen Hazen Wyman park (off State Route 86) in Painesville.

Almost half of the river's 67-mile length is open to upstream movements of fish. Harpersfield Dam, 45 stream miles inland, is the end of the line for spring and fall runs of trout and salmon. Anglers can get to the dam via State Rt. 534 south of Geneva, and public parks on both sides of the dam make for an easy go at the fishing.

From South Madison upstream to the dam, more than 20 miles of wadable stream awaits. Here, the Grand passes through flatlands in the upper reaches, but the banks gradually rise as the river flows toward the Madison area.

CHAGRIN RIVER. A five-foot-high dam at Daniels Park in Willoughby blocks upstream runs of most trout and salmon. Some steelhead and coho are taken above the dam, but the catchable fish in this heavily-stocked waterway are mainly found along the five-mile length of stream between the mouth and the dam.

The entire lower Chagrin is passable by boat, with access at the Chagrin River Boat Launch near the mouth. Shoreline anglers can gain access south of Willoughby at State Rt. 84 and wade downstream to the Rt. 2 bridge. The late-spring run of steelhead is good, but the word has been out for several seasons that the fall steelie run is better. Expect crowds of waders shortly after the first steelhead appear in this river.

ROCKY RIVER. The Rocky, at least the lower Rocky, is the most metropolitan of all major salmonid-supporting tributaries to Lake Erie. Located in the west suburbs of the City of Cleveland, the river lies within the Cleveland Metroparks System. The Rocky River Reservation (North) affords access to much of the lower river. The park's Valley Parkway leads to most of the good steelhead spots along that section of the river near the lake. A small section of the park's waters is open to boating, and fishermen can use the boat launch at the north end of the reservation.

Despite the proximity of a major city, the river runs through some remarkably unspoiled countryside. Farther upstream, riffles—not many quiet pools—beckon both spin and fly fishers in search of the leaping steelhead. This pursuit became so popular here that a steelhead organization was formed in 1984. Much more specific information about steelie locations can be gotten by writing to the Ohio Central Basin Steelheaders, P.O. Box 29577, Parma, Ohio 44129.

SANDUSKY RIVER. Warm-water species take over now that we have moved farther west into the shallow waters of the Western Basin and Sandusky Bay. Boaters and waders begin the walleye chase as soon as ice disappears from the bay and river. Later in the spring, good numbers of decent-sized (10- to 13-inch) white bass can be taken.

The harbor at the stream mouth is well protected by virtue of its location within sheltered Sandusky Bay. Boat traffic can move inland 16-20 miles, depending on water levels. The good shoreline fishing (both bank and wading) also extends that far inland.

Although not suitable for trout or salmon, some steelhead from eastern waters will find their way into the Sandusky. The real attraction, though, is the abundant walleye and white bass, plus the black bass and yellow perch, which greet anglers who have come to spend the day on the Sandusky.

MAUMEE RIVER. Spring is the prime season for this westernmost tributary in Ohio. The Maumee Bay area includes the city of Toledo, where anglers gather—elbow-to-elbow at times—in early spring. The walleye spawning run happens fast, and the news of its arrival travels even faster. Wading casters gather along every possible bank access and bridge crossing to cast an assortment of jigs, body baits and spoons in the direction of passing walleye. First-light hours are considered the best time to be on the river, but overcast days when wading traffic is minimal can keep the walleye biting all day long.

Heavy fishing pressure has been exerted on both Maumee Bay and the Maumee River each spring since pre-spawn walleye fishing first became popular in the early 80's. But Ohio fishery personnel believe that an open walleye season during the spawning period has not decreased walleye numbers. A visit to the banks of this river sometime in mid-March might confirm that claim. Taken are thousands of walleye well above the five-pound mark, and during peak periods many anglers walk off with a limit of these bigger fish. In recent years, the better catches have been taken by boaters working the shallows in the bay. The flotilla gradually moves up the bay as the fish near their spawning areas.

The river extends inland as far as Fort Wayne, but the better fishing is concentrated along the first 15 miles upstream from the lake. After the walleye run, more white bass than black bass or yellow perch can be found in Maumee waters. The black bass and yellow perch numbers are much greater in the open waters of the lake along the rocky shoals surrounding the islands.

Other Thoughts

Dozens of other highly fishable creeks and rivers can be found along the U.S. shoreline. Timing is everything, but which stream you fish may not be of supreme importance. Many trout and salmon run up into whatever tributary is at hand. That is, many salmonids do not imprint to a specific stream. At times, large cohos, kings and steelies have been seen finning in ditch-like brooks barely deep enough to cover them.

Stocking figures, available from the various states, should be studied to better understand possible fish movements in tributaries; however, at times, good trib fishing can be found in many of the smaller feeders that never received initial stockings of trout or salmon.

Wherever you choose to seek salmonids, keep in mind that all tribs are subject to changes in seasonal patterns from year to year. Variations in water levels, temperature changes, and rainfall runoff call for a re-reading of stream conditions each year. Warm, clear, low stream water during the early fall may delay a run of trout and salmon for weeks. On the other hand, normal weather patterns, with high water levels, may provide good fishing in streams that did not see fish a year earlier. Keep all options open when trib fishing. Many streams can offer up some pleasant surprises.

Chapter 19

The Methods

Some thirty or more miles upstream from Painesville, Ohio, in a setting that looks like a Currier & Ives Christmas card, Bill Baker sends out dry and wet flies all winter long in the upper reaches of the Grand River. Baker, an experienced fly tier and avid steelhead fisherman, spends much of his time along reaches of streams only a few feet wide and overhung with pine boughs and listing tree trunks and limbs.

Baker is one of a growing number of trib fishermen who are out all year and who vary their techniques as conditions warrant. He feels that there is almost always something that will work when the steelhead are in. He feels steelhead movements are influenced mainly by water temperatures, and he constantly moves up and down the Grand River (and many other tribs) in search of water temperatures that will attract and hold fish.

Steelhead are the number one tributary attraction around Lake Erie, and in the coming years, it is almost certain that they will dominate the tributary scene even more. Like Bill Baker, those who haunt the feeder streams here are increasingly enchanted with the thought of taking this great game fish on the long rod. But however one chooses to fish for steelhead, challenge is the word. The weather is cold, the fish are often picky, and when you do hook one it doesn't at all mean that you're going to land him.

In the preceding chapters, we discussed Erie's more prominent tributaries, and looked at Erie's tributary fishing as a whole. Here, we will focus completely on techniques and strategies for catching the main tributary game fish.

Before we get into the specific species, though, here are some general concepts.

It should be first said that just as the eastern and western areas of Erie differ from one another, so too do the eastern and western tributaries differ.

The Western Basin feeders are inhabited by warm-water species almost exclusively. Walleye, bass (smallmouth and largemouth), white and yellow perch, and other panfish call for entirely different tackle items than those needed for trout and salmon. The Eastern Basin feeders have some warm-water fish, but trout and salmon grab most of the headlines.

Salmonid seekers carry a vast assortment of live and/or natural baits, along with a generous selection of artificial offerings. The well-equipped tributary bait fisherman might carry live minnows; nightcrawlers and/or blood worms; egg sacks or skein sections; and grubs such as spikes, mousie grubs, oak-leaf grubs, etc. Artificial lures run the gamut, but the mainstays for casting are spinners and spoons. While crankbaits and floating stickbaits take fair numbers of stream-run trout and salmon, the greater numbers fall to medium to small-sized Mepps or Super Vibrax spinners; or Little Cleos, Kastmasters, Krocodiles, and other spoons capable of good wobbling movement in the current.

Western Basin trib tackle ranges from spoons and plugs for shore-casting immediately following ice-out to light bobbers for presenting suspended live bait in gentle, summer currents. The increased numbers of white bass and perch has generated an increase in light and ultralight tackle items: spoons, spinners and lead-head jigs. Jigs, in particular, have gone through extensive redesigns and modifications for use in light-tackle fishing. Today, the hair and feather jig is frequently augmented with vinyl, plastic and rubber bodies and tails to better entice fish in the shallow waters of bays and tributaries.

Smart Erie trib fishermen are always looking for patterns. The trick is to use this approach without becoming a slave to one pattern. At times, the best thing you can do is use some technique or lure that is totally outlandish, just because you feel like it. But more often, there will be some set of circumstances that you can observe and key in on.

More than one conservation officer here has told me the story. He walks a particular tributary checking licenses only to find that all the fishermen report taking fish on the same lure, bait or fly pattern worked at the same time up and down the waterway. For example, a chartreuse streamer may have been the ticket for an hour or two after sunrise the length of the stream. Then, an hour later, the ticket might have been a red-dyed spawn sack with an inch-long section of orange yarn. So often, the pattern will be there but one can't confirm it unless he speaks to many other anglers as he leaves the stream. Obviously, the roaming game warden is in an excellent position to see these patterns. And see them they do.

Anyone can luck onto the right pattern. The question is, how can you predict a pattern at the start of a day's fishing, so that you're using the right combination from the outset? It's not always easy, but it certainly pays to keep an angling log book so you can look back at what's worked. Almost all really successful fishermen keep notes, sometimes quite detailed ones.

Topping the list of most popular and most successful natural baits for all species of trout and salmon here has to be the well-tied egg sack. Blue-dyed sacks seem to draw the most attention at the start of the fall run; reds and oranges do well in the middle of the run; and chartreuse can be a top color later in the winter season.

On the Erie tribs, there are certain key factors you should pay attention to in your quest to predict what's going to work at such and such a time. Water temperature is of course of paramount importance. Hitting these tribs without a thermometer is a handicap you don't need. Bring one along, on all trips. One thing temperature might be able to tell you is whether to use lures or baits, assuming you're amenable to both approaches. For example, it is widely known that steelhead in the streams will take lures early in the run before water temperatures dip downward. When the water gets too cold, spawn sacks or other natural baits work much better on steelies. It's key to remember that it can take only a few degrees difference in water temperature to turn the fish one way or another.

Still on the subject of steelhead, temperatures upstream may be more favorable than those downstream. Or vice versa. Or, a stream may be in a favorable temperature range while another stream 20 miles to the west may not be.

Water level can be of supreme importance in the tributaries. Nearly all the experts, state biologists included, acknowledge that high water levels in the tribs are better than low ones. We don't want floods, of course. But there is no question that a good rainstorm can "bring the fish in" when the spawning run is about to commence. It is also very important to remember that unusually high water, most often prompted by rains, can bring certain fish into the tributaries even when it's not spawning season.

The amount of sunlight and clarity of the water are two interrelated factors. It is these two factors which determine light penetration in the water. Most anglers here have observed that overcast days often outproduce bright sunny days. If it's overcast and the water is a bit high and off-color, it could be an excellent day. The amount of light penetration in water is one of the factors that is apt to change most quickly. A clean, gravelly stream may clear up very quickly after a heavy rain, while a mud or silt-bottomed larger stream may take two or more days. The fishing can be greatly affected. Human activities can also affect stream clarity, not to mention stream levels. If there is a hydro dam on the stream you are fishing, water levels may fluctuate, and there may be specific times of the day or week to be on that stream...or to avoid it. It is broadly true that game fish are more apt to bite when they feel the least vulnerable to predators. And in general, they probably feel least vulnerable when the water is high enough and murky enough to conceal their presence.

There are of course exceptions to this. If a stream is very cold, a bright, sunny winter day might be just the medicine to make things pop. On such a day, the fishing may be best in mid-day or mid-afternoon when water temperatures are at their peak. This can be true even with species that are notably crepuscular (most active at dawn and dusk).

Bait fish movements are yet another thing to consider. One nice thing about stream fishing is that certain factors are more observable than they are out in the broad expanses of Erie itself. This is not always true with bait fish, however. Non-spawning fish will follow bait into the tribs, but depending on water depth and clarity, you may not witness these comings and goings. You can bet, though, that if a particular kind of bait moves into a certain trib at a certain time of the year, the chances are excellent that the pattern will repeat itself in subsequent years. It takes time on the water to learn about fish movements, but while you're garnering that sure-to-be-hard-won knowledge, you can talk to as many other fishermen and tackle store owners as possible.

Catching Steelhead

Some of the most traveled sport fishermen in North America consider the steelhead to be one of the top two game fish, the other being the Atlantic salmon. And there are those who believe the steelhead to be number one. As it's often been pointed out, the steelhead is widely available to anglers of modest means, while the Atlantic salmon is often available only to "sports" who can afford to travel to Canada and then pay the often weighty rod and guide fees. "Poor man's salmon" is a term appropriately applied to the steelhead.

Steelies are caught in Lake Erie but most are caught in the tribs. With the exception of the newer strains that are being experimented with, steelies are in the tribs mainly from October through April; they are a winter-run fish. Some experts believe that November and April are the top months. Others feel that the dead of winter is the best time, and if it's snowing, all the better. Anglers are usually "on" the steelies as soon as the runs begin, which is usually October or early November. Conversely, anglers pay somewhat less homage to the spring run from March through April.

From late October through much of November, steelhead are quite readily taken with lures and it is at this time, when the water temperature is still less than frigid, that the fish fight the hardest. As winter wears on, there is little question that natural baits work better. Taking a steelhead on a fly, most often a streamer or "steelhead fly", is a challenge at any time. That's mainly because the fish hold tight to the bottom and getting a fly down to the bottom presents its own set of difficulties.

Spin fishermen outnumber fly fishermen by a considerable margin. And, in general, baits outproduce lures by a good measure. While flyrods and reels are classic, most steelheaders prefer spinning gear. A medium to lightweight spinning rod and an egg sack is a tough combination to beat. Anglers using such a combo cast into the lake near tributary mouths; they fish in and around trib mouths; and they fish the tribs themselves, sometimes as much as 20 or 30 miles inland. Steelhead can and will travel inland until a fixed barrier stops them. Generally, the farther inland you go the smaller the water and the more intimate the setting. But it is probably true that the majority of steelhead running up from Erie are caught in the bottom five or ten miles of most tribs that in fact support a run.

Egg sacks are the number one bait. Both salmon and trout eggs are used, but in many places it is illegal to sell trout eggs in any form. Check on local regulations.

You can make up your own sacks or buy them in tackle stores. A sack is comprised of six or seven salmon eggs tied up in a little cheesecloth-like bag. The eggs themselves can be dyed, but usually the color of the sack is determined by the color of the cloth. Sack material is available in all colors: red, pink, chartreuse, orange and even blue. Sacks are usually fished on a short shank hook. Sizes four and six are popular, but some anglers go one hook size larger or smaller. Weight in the form of medium to large size split shot is almost always used. The bait must be presented very close to the bottom; it's one of the main keys in steelhead success.

Salmon eggs are much larger and give off slightly more scent during prolonged use. Trout eggs are finer and tend to break up faster in current, but they firm up when conditioned and take dye coloring quickly. Conditioning of fish eggs is not complicated. Unless eggs are taken streamside for immediate use, at-home preparation is simple. As soon as the two egg sacks are removed from the body cavity, cut segments to desired sizes and let them dry on paper toweling for a few hours. Borax and dye or a commercial preparation such as Pro-Cure will lock in color and firm up the egg segments. A large chunk of eggs will hold in strong currents through many casts. Still, gentle retrieves and casting motions are necessary to prevent the skein from coming apart or falling off the hook.

Color selection for skein is yet another matter of debate. Red, orange, yellow and natural are all argued for with equal vigor. An alternative to the chore of dying your eggs many different colors is a pocket filled with several different spools of dyed yarn. Just a small length of yarn looped above the skein will provide a spot of color and, hopefully, catch the eye of a gamefish. Skein, if it holds up and gives off the right scent track, can draw strikes once fish see the combination drifting along in the current or settling into a nearly calm pool.

The yarn ball is yet another great innovation recently introduced to winter steelhead fishing. Some experts argue that a yarn ball in the right size and color does not need to be masked with any kind of scent. Others assert that artificial offerings, especially in cold, clear waters, need all the masking they can get. Berkley's Strike, Fish Formula and other scent products mixed specifically for trout and salmon are used by some Erie trib fishermen.

Rubber and plastic eggs sold under many commercial names are used for steelhead. These can be found in assorted sizes and colors. Sometimes, a small marshmallow is added to one of these rubber eggs. The marshmallow gives off a milky trail that may help the offering to further simulate a real trout or salmon egg. There are days when these "fake foods" will draw more strikes than natural sack or skein offerings.

Speaking of Mouths

River and stream mouths are mainly a spring but mostly fall thing. The spring flurry can be quite brief, while the fall run can be both more intense and somewhat longer in duration. Note that we're not speaking of steelhead here, but rather, the other salmonid species: cohos, browns, and some chinooks.

When the stream mouths turn on, Erie's wall, pier and bank fishermen all have their day in the sun. Wading is also possible in some of the "estuaries."

Ice-out will find many casters chucking out relatively heavy, wind-resistant spoons such as Kastmasters, Cleos and KO Wobblers. Color combinations that have established themselves include silver/blue, silver/chartreuse and sometimes orange. In spring, rainbow and brown trout and king and coho salmon are the game fish most apt to be encountered at the mouths. The trout average 2-6 pounds and the salmon about 2-8 pounds with some fish exceeding ten pounds. Regrettably, the spring run is sometimes over before many fishermen even hear about it.

Fall in the estuaries is something to talk about, however. During some cool summers, the trout and salmon will start moving around the entrances to feeder mouths in late August. Greeting the pink but chilly sunrise can pay big dividends, as the first hour is the best hour for this type of fishing. A second-best situation is overcast days. On leaden or even stormy days, action may continue on and off all day long.

Specific location may not always matter too much. Near the magnet of a fall river mouth, the pier, breakwater, or stream or lake bank may all be good choices. The exact preferred location—if there is one—will vary somewhat from stream to stream.

Even a stream as small as Canadaway Creek, just west of Dunkirk, New York, will see 50 or more people gathered from the mouth up to the first bridge (Route 5) when the coho and rainbow trout begin their run in early to mid-fall. Both lures and bait will be used. Some trout go for a live minnow, but most fish are taken with some form of fish eggs such as sacks or skein portions. Resourceful mouth-area anglers use two rods. One is baited up and propped on a stick; and the other is used to cast spoons or spinners (more typically, spoons).

The length of the fall run varies, but the peak period generally lasts about two weeks. If possible, get there at the beginning of the run so you can get yourself tuned into the baits, lures, colors etc. that seem to be working. Since the run can occur at different times from year to year, you have little choice but to keep your eyes and ears open and keep up a dialogue with your local bait and tackle store. Outdoor columns in local newspapers can also key you in to the start of the good fishing.

Don't overlook shoreline trolling in and around trib mouths at this time of year. Shallow and mid-running casting lures can sometimes be hooked to long lines or Luhr Jensen's Hot Shot sideplaner—a lightweight device for getting relatively small lures out to the side of the boat in somewhat shallow waters. Hot Shots, Hot'n Tots, long stick-baits and many other shallow-running crankbaits will provide the wild movement that represents an injured bait fish trying to right itself. These near-surface trolling items sometimes draw incoming fish to the surface, resulting in exciting strikes and battles.

Part Four

Care of the Catch

Chapter 20

For Keeps

Although Lake Erie is situated among northern states known for their cold winters, summertime fishing excursions call for rapid cooling of fish. The trick here is to quickly do the admiring and picture-taking and then get the fish into the cooler to prevent spoilage.

Tributary fishermen here have it somewhat easier as the better stream fishing occurs during the cooler months of spring and fall. Then, too, shore fishermen can more quickly get the catch home or to a base location where there is refrigeration.

Some Preliminary Thoughts

Gut your fish as soon as it's feasible to do so. Here, though, you'll have to be careful not to break the law. Almost all states have become more stringent in the area of fish-cleaning laws. The states bordering Lake Erie vary in this regard. Study up so you know what your options are before you head out on the water.

Whether or not you were able to immediately "dress" (remove

entrails of) your fish, put it on ice as quickly as possible. In cold weather this isn't necessary, but you need some way to hold the fish in any case and it might as well be a cooler. Drain the cooler periodically. Fish should not sit in melted ice water in the cooler, although a short period of this would not do any harm.

Cooler size is something worth looking at. On those great lakes where very large king salmon and other large salmonids are commonly boated, a cooler of 100 quarts or larger is desirable. Erie's bounty runs a little smaller so an 80-quart cooler should be adequate. Unless you're really pessimistic, don't go smaller than 50 quarts. Perch and other panfishermen can live with coolers even a bit smaller than this.

Block ice lasts much longer. On the other hand, cube ice can be scattered around a fish to cool it more quickly. A good ploy is to bring both a block of ice and a large bag of cubes. The main thing, though, is to bring enough.

One tip worth mentioning is skin removal. Freshwater fish meat—

especially the meat of those large walleye, pike and salmonids—tends to absorb unpleasant flavors from skin. The skin is usually left on, though, when you'll be smoking the fish or cooking it on the grill.

In the past, Lake Erie fillets were prepared (commercially or in the kitchens of avid anglers) with the skin left on but the scales removed. Blue pike, perch and other panfish species were scaled and then either filleted or deheaded and gutted. Some cooks still prefer the skin left on for cooking, believing that it somehow helps retain flavor or at least juices. However, fish consumption advisories related to decreasing contaminants in fish almost universally recommend removal of the skin. The public has caught on.

Skinning or scaling the fish is not something you're liable to do on the boat; it's a dockside or kitchen table procedure, depending on what laws you're dealing with. But at-home preparation should include a few additional steps.

As soon as you've cut your fillets or steaks, quickly rinse these to eliminate all traces of blood, slime or internal body fluids. If the fish is to be left whole—for either cooking or freezing—do the same thing. In either case, after the quick rinsing, drain your fish or fish pieces on paper towels, to dry thoroughly. If the fish is to be eaten that day, the above steps should ideally be done immediately prior to the actual cooking. If some delay will occur, cover the fish or fish pieces tightly with some sort of wrap and place them on a plate in the refrigerator.

If you're planning to freeze all or part of your catch, wrap in small portions in a double thickness or wax paper or freezer paper. Then place in a plastic bag, squeeze out the air, and add a twist-tie. Inside, place a piece of paper with the date, contents, and how many people can be served by each portion within the bag.

The Stringer Question

Dig out any old fish pictures and invariably there will be a person or persons (usually male) holding up a batch of big lunkers on a stringer, chain or length of cable. There is nothing wrong with a deserved boast from time to time—it had been stamped into the angler's psyche that proof is in the dead fish pictures after an outing on the lake. The "biggest fish" contests still exist and the stringers can still be seen hanging over the gunwales of some boats, but times and fish-keeping techniques are gradually changing.

Stringers certainly are convenient; you simply hang the fish over the side. Also, where the law allows such practice, stringering permits culling. That is, a fisherman may catch a larger fish and cull or release a smaller fish which had been caught earlier.

Stringers, however, should only be used when waters are cool (say below 50 degrees) and their use should be confined to as short a period as possible. In waters above 50 degrees, any fish that have died on the stringer will begin deteriorating rapidly.

Fisheries biologists say that hooking mortality of stringered fish that have been released markedly increases in warmer water. What, then, are the other options?

Many states have enacted laws that fish must remain intact while the fisherman is on the water. New York, for example, has recently passed a fish cleaning law which requires that certain species may only be "gilled and gutted...while upon the waters of the state." Pennsylvania imposes an even stricter fish cleaning regulation known as the "point of consumption" law. This law mandates that fish not be cleaned until they have been removed from the water and transported to wherever the fish will be stored or consumed. What this means is that much care has to go into keeping large fish intact for later cleaning.

Live Well Limits

Live wells perform essentially the same function as stringers but have the same limitations when the water's surface temperature rises above 50 degrees. When surface temperatures are cool, a live well fitted with the proper size aerator can keep fish alive all day long. Unlike stringers, which pull fish through the water and cause either hyperventilation or strangulation, a good-sized live well (one with a capacity of 50 quarts or more) is capable of keeping a five-fish limit of walleye alive and uninjured until the end of the trip when the fish are to be cleaned.

The problem for Lake Erie's boating fishermen who plan to keep

A good way to cut down on the cost of ice: Fill plastic bottles with water and freeze them before your trip. The squarish ones are better as they nestle into the corners of the cooler more effectively.

their catch is that many of the larger fish are caught during the warmer months of the year when live well intakes draw warm surface water into the holding tank. Cold-water species (trout and salmon) will not remain alive more than a half hour even in a well-aerated live well when water temperatures reach 60 degrees. Warm-water species (walleye, yellow perch and other panfish) will not remain alive in live wells when water temperatures rise into the mid-60's.

When spring and fall fishing seasons are at their peak, a live well can be the most convenient and efficient means of keeping fish for later consumption. But frequent checks must be made on the condition of the held fish. All fish which show signs of weakness (i.e. belly-up or at the surface on its side) should be removed and immediately placed in a well-chilled cooler.

Clearly, both stringers and live wells have their limitations. In most cases, if your fish are destined for the dinner table, you just can't beat a well-iced cooler.

Coolers Become Hot

"Fish boxes" are a centerpiece somewhere in the aft deck on party boats in salt water ports and aboard the head boats along the Great Lakes. Charter boat operators know that they will lose clients if their catch arrives home in a less than edible state. Thus, party boats keep large, fish-holding boxes ready for the moment when fish are brought on deck.

We've already said a few things about coolers earlier in this chapter. Now we'll add just a few other tips.

Whether built into the hull of the boat or of a portable, carry-on design, a cooler should have a white or light-colored lid to reduce heating from the sun's rays. Also, it's not a bad idea to place a small block of ice or freezer pack in the cooler the night before an outing so that the liner is allowed to cool. The principle is the same here as pre-heating a Thermos with hot water.

Square-cornered plastic gallon and half-gallon containers of water can be frozen and used as ice blocks. Their shape allows them to fit into the corners of the cooler and provides more room for those days of good fortune when the big fish are hitting better than usual. What's more, when the ice in the container starts melting it does not create a build-up of water as would plastic-wrapped cubes or blocks, but it does provide a cold drink.

Cleaning a cooler after each use assures that the next catch will not pick up odors left from the previous trip. A mild solution of bleach left in the cooler overnight will usually remove most fish odors. Avoid premature cracking and deterioration of the cooler's inside liner by pouring water into the cooler before adding bleach. A mild solution (one-half cup of bleach per gallon of water) is enough to clean even the largest of coolers. Be sure not to mix a household soap/cleanser and bleach at the same time. When soap and bleach are used together, the two chemicals can seriously damage liners of the most durable coolers. Check with your cooler's manufacturer for specialized cleaning instructions. When washed and then bleached in a two-stage cleaning operation, fish coolers do not retain foul odors. Even though most coolers can withstand a two-stage cleaning, first with soap followed by a soaking with bleach and water, it is still a good idea to pour out the bleach/water solution the next day and invert the cooler with the lid open to allow it to air dry.

A well-kept cooler means well-kept fish. The end result will be enjoyable eating.

Chapter 21

To Fight Another Day

Line tangles, bad weather, unfavorable water conditions and difficulty in just finding the fish: It's the usual state of the Great Lakes fisherman. Unlike the more chartable, and somewhat more predictable waters of inland lakes, ponds and small feeder streams, the Great Lakes and their tributaries are large, changeable and difficult to get a handle on.

Then comes one of those rare days when everything clicks and coolers or buckets get filled to capacity, or near-capacity. These are the times when proper catch-and-release techniques are important and can actually add to the enjoyment of the sport. Sometime, not determined by limits legally imposed, there comes a point when there is still time to fish but there are more than enough fish on board to please everyone. For example, the yellow perch and the walleye fisheries in Erie have now improved to a point where overkill is a distinct possibility on many occasions.

While many Lake Erie fishermen do fish for food, and often attempt to take and clean enough to "get through the winter," some outings result in more fish than can be used. Also, when larger specimens of any fish (especially perch) start hitting, many anglers begin to "cull" and let all the little ones go.

A New Release on Life

The catch-and-release movement has been slow to be adopted on Lake Erie, because so many of the popular species are highly desirable food fish: trout, salmon, walleye, yellow perch, white perch, bass and others. Historically, Lake Erie was selectively fished by Native Americans, followed by European settlers who almost exclusively gathered fish from Lake Erie with nets. Both of these groups fished for food—period.

During the developing years of the nineteenth century, commercial fishing reigned. Hook-and-line efforts were confined mainly to the shoreline and even more frequently to the feeder streams and rivers along the lake.

Sport fishermen in any great numbers did not begin working the open waters of Lake Erie until the early twentieth century. They began appearing in competition with commercial netters when the catches of blue pike were high. In fact, many fisheries managers and veteran observers look back at the early development of "sport fishing" as not much more than a harvesting of meat for the table. The heavy lines used to catch these relatively small fish was strong enough to assure success and maximize yield. There wasn't much that was "sporting" about it.

The only fish which might possibly be released back then were either too small, diseased, or of an undesired species—those considered inedible. Yet the concept of releasing fish has slowly but certainly come to Lake Erie. Excessive numbers of all kinds of fish are being released in greater numbers each year.

One of the most detrimental expressions in all of fish talk may be the one about "throwing a fish back." Bad grammar aside, the assumption that a fish tossed back into the water will live to fight another day is not always correct.

Hooked fish are vulnerable to injury. Fishery biologists tell us that all fish, even the most ferocious hitters and fighters, can suffer serious injury to internal organs when dropped onto the water surface. Many fish which swim away energetically and seemingly intact suffer what biologists term "hooking mortality." These fish die as much as eight hours later. Along with the blood loss as a result of hook removal, internal injuries leave many of these fish fatally weakened.

Clearly, "throwing" is out. Properly placing a fish back—should the fish be removed from the water in the first place—gives that fish a greater chance for survival.

How the fish re-enters the water is most important. The U.S. Fish and Wildlife Service, along with several state agencies, recommends the "head-first-plunge" release. That is, gently lift the fish with one hand under the front section of the belly but not inside the gill covers and the other hand between the vent and the tail. Lift the fish over the side of the boat and very close to the water and then vigorously plunge the fish into the water head-first directly toward the bottom. This release allows water to pass through the gills and speed up a return to normal breathing. One of the most vulnerable of all Lake Erie fish is the lake trout, which is generally caught in deeper water and suffers from extreme water pressure changes when brought to the surface. This head-first-plunge release is especially suited to lakers, which need help to return unharmed to their preferred habitat at or near the lake bottom.

While the landing net remains a necessary tackle item aboard any fishing vessel, fish intended for release might do better if let go somewhere in or near the surface of the water, without being lifted into the boat and placed on the floor during hook removal. Most smaller fish can be firmly gripped from above at the point where the gill covers end. Bass can be briefly immobilized with a firm grip on the lower jaw, but don't try this method with walleye or members of the pike family. Long-nosed pliers or hook disgorgers make it much easier to quickly remove the hook and have the fish returned and moving back to its chosen cover.

In-water hook removal is sometimes possible. It's done to protect fish from the many unseen injuries suffered when the catch is rolled around in a net, put on a hard floor while the hook is taken out and finally held in midair before being put back overboard. Each of these steps further stresses the fish and increases the chances of it dying later.

Continued bleeding well after the hook has been removed increases the likelihood that the fish will not survive. Consider keeping the bleeding smaller fish even though a larger fish might be caught later. Ethics go beyond rules and regulations and responsible behavior is more important than a fish count at day's end.

Whether the motive is culling smaller fish or a pure catch-and-release philosophy, a prompt, in-the-water release of the hooked fish considerably increases its chances for survival.

Too Heavy on the Ultralights?

How much is "just enough"?

Ultralight tackle saw its ascendency in the early 70's and its peak somewhere in the mid-80's. Much has been learned about the necessity to reduce line dimensions and lure weights so that terminal tackle (jigs, spoons, spinners and body baits) can simulate natural forage in various states of vulnerability.

Tackle manufacturers started to design and produce rods and reels with extreme sensitivity and the ability to cast light lures to greater distances. The movement lasted long enough and the competition was strong enough to bring the price of smooth, durable, light-tackle rigs into the hands of the average fisherman.

Many are the fish taken from weed edges and shallow shoal structures that would not have fallen for presentations made with heavier tackle. But when does light tackle become too light? One example is when a fisherman fights a trout or muskellunge for more than an hour just to say that the fish was brought in on two- or four-pound test line. If this fish were to be released, in the name of sport, its chances of survival would be poor. Biologists point to the buildup of toxins in the system of a fish when it is continually brought to the surface and repeatedly struggles to regain its place at or near the bottom.

Clearly, modern anglers are not going to revert to very heavy rods and very heavy lines. At times, lighter lines fool more fish. At times, lighter rods detect the light hits of moody feeders. At times, a light spinning or casting rod is all that is needed to either cast a certain distance, play a certain fish, or deal with a particular situation.

Somewhere between a wispy, ultralight spinning rod and the solid backbone of a no-nonsense casting rod lies the rod for the everyday fisherman interested in catching a few fish without either snapping them off or killing the ones to be released by overplaying them. It's a balance of philosophy as much as a balance of tackle.

Four-pound test line works well for perch in the shallows. With larger spreaders and greater depths, six-pound test might work better. Many flat-liners claim that they never use more than six-pound test line when going for walleyes—even fish in the five- to eight-pound class. But a river troller after pike or muskies would probably be going light with either 10- or 12-pound test line on the spool.

Judgement is greater than prescriptions. When the tackle becomes too light, move up to a slightly higher line weight. It can be a very big factor in successfully releasing fish to fight another day.

Chapter 22

The Tables on Cooking

very book on fishing seems to conclude with a batch of recipes
in which precise ingredients and methods are listed. Yet every
good cook ends up by "doctoring" or "sweetening to taste." In
light of this, we here include a few descriptions of cooking procedures
which should help across the board. Since Lake Erie's two most popular species, yellow perch and walleye, are also top tablefare, the
business of preparation becomes pure pleasure.

Fillets: Watching Your Waste

Many an experienced angler and fish cleaner has lamented that
woefully too much of the meat ends up being put out with the
garbage. Careless cleaning techniques and neglect of edible meat
sections cause waste—but it doesn't have to be that way.

Filleting fish represents the completing of the circle. It's a pleas-
ing operation that reaffirms the skill and perseverance of the angler.
It also has a direct, tangible outcome: a fine meal for both the angler
and his invited guests. In sharing the bounty of a renewable resource,

the fisherman's dedication to his avocation is also renewed.

Along with this positive attitude about filleting, some pointers may help to improve results:

1. Use a quality fillet knife and keep it sharp at all times. Both in filleting and skinning, a sharp edge means cleaner, more precise cuts. It may also mean less slips and possible accidents as the result of hacking through skin and bones to get at the meat.

2. Bones are knife guides. Learn the peculiar bone structure of each fish, since they vary. Cuts should ideally be made parallel to bone alignments. To put it another way, as you sweep the blade, the individual bones should be perpendicular to the blade.

3. Sawing means it's time to resharpen. When the blade dulls to a point that you have to saw to cut, stop and lightly put a fine edge (less than 10 degrees) on it. Or, use a few leather stropping strokes to maintain that fine cutting edge. These "touch up" sharpenings should not be as lengthy as when rehoning and should only involve the metal surfaces along the cutting edge—the first bevel.

4. Keep the blade in the area of fish meat, avoiding contact with bones, the outer surface of skin, and the table surface. Theoretically, the edge of a filleting knife should touch nothing but meat. It's a good idea to use a second, stronger-edged knife for making the initial cuts and for cutting skin, bone and fins when that's necessary.

The greatest amount of meat loss usually occurs around the perimeter of the rib cage and the protruding part of the vertebrae at the midsection. Some choose to slice through the ribs and then go back to remove the rib bones as the fillet is lying skin-side down. Others make a vertical cut which stops just short of the ribs while detaching that meat from the top of the fish to the lateral line. Here, once the entire strip of top meat is loosened a second pass is made with the knife below the lateral line and from the tail towards the outer rib cage. This second approach takes a few more seconds per fish, but it assures more meat per fillet.

Externally, two additional pieces of removable meat are often discarded: cheeks and gill bases. Nearly everyone who hangs around a fisherman long enough learns about taking out the cheek pieces. Larger panfish and almost every edible gamefish has a small piece of "soft tissue" just above the end of its mouth. These cheek pieces lift out with a gentle, circular motion of the tip of a knife, preferably a rounded knife.

One delicacy overlooked by all but a select few is the gill base—that rough triangle which is at the base of the gills and which includes the pectoral fin. The removal of this section (there is one on each side of the fish) calls for a firm twist and some washing and scraping to remove small scales. Also, this piece of meat contains several fine bones which must be picked out after steaming. Most anglers familiar with this delicacy only prepare the gill bases when cleaning fish for immediate consumption. Several species can be used, but large walleye are the best. The sweet flavor of the meat is well worth the extra effort.

Sweeten the Catch

Of the many challenges faced by fishing folk, trying to interest non-fisherpersons in sharing the catch is high on the list. It can take more than a tad of culinary prowess to win over those skeptics who don't like fish because it tastes "fishy."

Assuming all the proper handling and storage steps have been followed, the best thing you can do is this: Serve the fish as fresh as possible. The same day is best. Always avoid freezing when you can serve the fish fresh instead.

One highly effective method for preparation is described in an article by R.L. Ball which appeared in the Sept. 1990 issue of *The Bucket*, Official Publication of the S.O.N.S. (S.O.N.S. stands for "Save Our Native Species.")

Want to get rid of "fishy taste?" Take a tip from the pros. Gaminess is a wonderful trait when a fish is on the line, but gaminess on the serving platter is a totally different matter. Unfortunately, many of our finest sportfish suffer from some distinct culinary shortcomings. Trout, salmon, shad, mackerel, bluefish, and many other species are excessively oily to some tastes. Pike, pickerel, catfish, and many other species tend to taste overly fishy. Most freshwater fish—including black bass, bluegill, and crappie—have wonderful flavor when taken from clean water, but often taste like the lake bottom when caught from less than pristine habitats.

You can cure all these problems by soaking your pan-dressed fish or fil-

lets overnight in a simple salt-and-soda solution. Many of the best restaurants and hotel chefs have been "sweetening" fish this way for decades, but few sportsmen seem to know the trade secret.

Measure three tablespoons of table salt and two teaspoons of baking soda into one gallon of cold water and stir until thoroughly dissolved. Submerge the fish in this solution, weigh them down with a heavy plate, and refrigerate overnight, or for at least six hours.

When the soaking is completed, you'll find that the brine is covered with a floating layer of oil and gelatinous slime. Since these are the substances that transmit most of the "off" flavors found in fish, their removal will make almost any variety of gamefish taste sweeter and fresher, but not all that bland.

Discard the used saltwater, and rinse the fish under cold tap water. Let them drip dry on paper towels, and then cook according to your favorite recipe or freeze them for later use.

When family members who "don't like" fish begin asking for seconds, you'll become a permanent convert to the salt-and-soda method.

Fired Up About Smoking

Before modern freezing and refrigeration, smoking meat and fish was the principal means of preserving those foods where salt was unavailable or too expensive. A brief tour around the grounds of Mt. Vernon, home base of our nation's father, George Washington, shows the importance of smoking during the formative years of the United States of America.

Washington's smokehouse was the size of a modest cottage, and the center smoking area allowed for large, suspended cuts of meats: hams, roasts and strips of jerky. But all around the outside of the smoking area can be seen racks for placing fish that were freshly taken from the Potomac. Generally, fish did not take as long as animal meats to cure; it lasted longer, important back then; and, as we well know today, provided substantial protein without much fat.

Refrigeration and various other methods of long-term food preservation could have made smoking fish a thing of our historical past. Yet something there is that loves the smell of smoked fish. When batches of fish come from the home smoker today, there is little worry about them taking up space in the refrigerator. When the tray is set out and the aroma gets around, little is left for storage. The taste is as good as the smell, too.

There are basically three methods for smoking fish: cold smoking, flame smoking and baking with "liquid smoke."

Cold smoking has become a relic. This method requires that the meat or fish be placed in racks in some kind of enclosure away from the direct source of heat and smoke. A duct transfers the smoke into the enclosure and the meat is slowly coated and seasoned—most meats take more than 24 hours to be fully processed. The problem with this system is that meat may spoil in the process if not carefully attended. With cold smoking, thoroughness is essential but not easy to assess.

Flame smoking has the advantage of allowing the chef greatest flexibility in controlling the variables, such as relative dryness or moistness, flavoring, and size of pieces to be smoked. Inexpensive, portable smokers can be set up in the smallest of back yards, and the options for seasonings are boundless. There is a distinct flavor for each of the hardwood chips used in finishing off a batch of smoked fish. (Avoid using even the driest of pine, spruce or other softwoods.) Tip: Liquid smoke, described next, can be lightly brushed on meat sections at any stage of smoking.

Liquid smoke products have been available for a decade and have just recently caught on with busy fish smokers. The product contains the same ingredients which are used in commercially processed foods sold in food stores as "smoked." Many states have banned the sale of air-smoked food items, but the liquid-smoking process is acceptable.

The distinct advantage of liquid smoke is speed. While a flame smoker may take four to eight hours to fully cook the thicker cuts of fish meat, liquid smoke takes about an hour in an oven set low (250 degrees).

Some householders complain about the odor created when fish are baked with a coating of liquid smoke. Should that be the case, consider doing the fillets on a sheet of foil placed on the backyard covered barbecue grill. Set the flame on its lowest setting and check the rack every few minutes. Remove the fillets when all the juices have drained from the fillets and most of the liquid has evaporated on the foil. Most batches take about an hour of grilling. At that point, the fillets should have a light or darkening coat of brown and be fully cooked.

Note that there is no need to flip the fillets while they are smoking on a covered grill.

Frying Tackle

Every fish chef has his favorite frying formula. It might include a particular type of oil (like peanut), certain pet seasonings, beer batter, a certain type of coating, and the list goes on. Here are a few suggestions to elevate fish frying in a health-conscious world.

Thinning is one means of consistent cooking. Big walleye fillets tend to end up either overcooked or underdone, with the thicker sections of meat loaded with cooking oil. To avoid these problems with fillets of bigger fish, place the fillets skin side down and slice the fillets parallel with the cutting surface to a thickness of less than one inch. Then separate the skin from the meat with a very sharp fillet knife.

"Batter check" is a basic step for both professional and home cooks going the deep-fry route. It is a way to check the temperature of the oil in which you will do the deep frying. 375-400 degrees is about right, but if you don't have a thermometer to use for the purpose, drop into the cooking oil a small sample of your batter coated fish. It should remain afloat, bubbling and dancing around on the surface. If not, wait until the oil gets a little hotter. Usually, the correct point is just below smoking. Caution: Once a heavy layer of cooking oil soaks into your fish, usually as a result of too-low oil temperature, no amount of baking or draining will remove the excess.

However, the "micro-bakeoff" technique can somewhat reduce the amount of cooking oil absorbed by deep-fried fillets. After removing pieces of deep-fried fish (any species) from cooking oil, place them on a paper towel on a plate and place the batch in a microwave oven on a low setting for two to four minutes. The meat stays moist and much more cooking oil is drained off this way than when drained on a rack.

Brought to a Boil

As in all cooking methods, the fish for boiling should be as fresh as possible and cut up as little as possible until cooking commences. Cut the meat into one-inch strips or squares and have the water up to a rolling boil. Place the fish pieces in the boiling water in batches small enough so that the boiling does not stop. Cooking takes less than three minutes. In another pot, have lemon slices immersed in melted butter and heated to a point just below boiling. Thoroughly drain the pieces of fish and then pour the lemon/butter sauce over them. A minute or two in the microwave set at low power will further soak the butter sauce into the fish.

Panfish Dishes

Every small fillet taken from Lake Erie can be tastefully prepared and enjoyed. David O. Kelch, Area Extension Agent of the Ohio Sea Grant, has earned a reputation for the diverse ways he has of preparing sheepshead (freshwater drum.) Opinions vary all around the lake as to the desirability of the drum, but few will argue with the advice given in Fact Sheets #23 & 24 authored by Kelch.

Kelch has assembled many recipes for preparing sheepshead, as well as other more popular gamefish and panfish frequently caught in Lake Erie. His "Fillets Italian Style" calls for oven baking in a seasoned tomato sauce. The broiling recipe includes a generous coating of catsup, lemonade concentrate, one clove of finely chopped garlic and four crushed bay leaves. Fact Sheets 23 and 24 contain many more fish-preparation suggestions and are available from Ohio Sea Grant Advisory Service, 484 W. 12th Ave., Columbus, Ohio 43210.

'Tis The Seasoning

Powerful seasoning requires tactful application. Although seasoning is the key to making good fish taste better, too much of a strong seasoning added to any fish will overpower its natural flavor.

Seasonings such as cloves, minced garlic, Italian seasonings (oregano, basil and mild peppers) and flavored cheeses all perk up fish dinners, when these seasonings are used properly. One interesting spice blend is Old Bay Seasoning. This product, long associated with

Chesapeake Bay and used mainly with shellfish, works well with fresh-water fish. It should be sprinkled thinly and evenly so that strong flavoring is not built up in parts of the fish.

One recipe which rarely appears in the cook books is fish lasagna. It can be done different ways but here's how we do it. In a lightly oiled baking pan (experts go with peanut oil) alternate layers of thin fillets lightly coated with seasoned breading and single layers of sliced Swiss, American or other cheese of your choice. Continue layering to within a half inch of the top of the pan. Apply seasonings as desired on the top layer of fish. Bake in a preheated oven at 375 degrees until the cheese begins to brown...about 30-45 minutes. Juices should begin evaporating and breading should absorb the remaining fish juices and flavors. Sauces for this fish lasagna can be either red (toma-to) or white (cream and cheese mixes), but the sauces should be prepared separately and served on the side. This way, the fish bakes to a point where its juices begin to evaporate and the meat doesn't become mushy soft.

And here is the final fish-cooking suggestion: Every piece of fish is worth saving. When overzealous cooks bake, broil or boil more pieces of fish than are eaten at the first sitting, break the remaining fish into fine pieces and try it in the same mix prepared for tuna sal-ads and spreads. The mild flavor of most freshwater fish mixed with mayonnaise, pepper, onion, salad dressings and seasonings makes for interesting sandwich spreads and pate-like dip dishes.

Afterword

The reader may have noticed that, to this point, little mention has been made of the current problems facing Lake Erie. Like the other Great Lakes, Erie has some very real ones.

PCB's, DDT, Chlordane, Dieldrin, Mirex—these are some of the well known and notorious toxic chemicals that have made their way into the Great Lakes over the years. Every one of these has been found in the tissues taken from Erie fish, but at present, levels are low enough—in some cases barely detectable—that Lake Erie fish are generally considered safe to eat.

The New York State Department of Health posts no general warning against eating fish taken from Lake Erie, although Erie does fall under this state's general advisory to "eat no more than one–half pound of fish per week from any water in New York." In the current (1990–1991) *New York State Fishing Regulations Guide*, Erie is not even mentioned in that section labelled "Health Advisory." This is in noticeable contrast to Lake Ontario, on which there are a number of warnings concerning the eating of fish.

Neither do Pennsylvania or Ohio post any general advisories against the eating of Lake Erie fish. Ohio does impose restrictions on fishing in certain bays and river mouth areas, however.

A second type of problem is what is commonly referred to as "Ballast Bums", undesirable aquatic lifeforms that made their way into the

Great Lakes chain after certain canal systems connected these fresh water bodies to the sea. More than 50 such foreign invaders have been documented in the five Great Lakes, but only a relative few are cause for significant concern. The most notable are B.C.'s, sea lampreys and the most recent menace, zebra mussels.

Bythothrephes cederstroemi, usually referred to as B.C.'s or water fleas, are found throughout the Great Lakes. Some scientists think that this tiny (0.4 inch long) organism can cause disruption in the food chain, while others think it may actually fit into the web of life here. No final statement has yet been made on B.C.'s and their impact on Great Lakes fisheries.

The ballast bum with the longest tenure in the Great Lakes is the sea lamprey, a parasitic eel–like fish which preys on other fish, including desirable game fish. Lake trout were particularly hard hit by this voracious and persistent blood–sucking creature. Using lampricides to attack the creature in and around its spawning sites, scientists have made strong inroads against the lamprey, but it's doubtful that this parasite will ever be totally eradicated.

The menace that is the zebra mussel came vividly into the homes of millions of Americans recently when public television aired a major documentary about the Great Lakes. When these mollusks began making their way into Lake Erie via the Detroit River in 1988, a fairly significant panic ensued. Extremely prolific, this hard–shelled organism can spread rapidly as it coats, in sprawling colonies, almost any submerged object. Some intake pipes of utility companies, for example, have been almost totally clogged up in waters where the zebra mussel occurs, including in Lake Erie. There is little question that the zebra mussel holds the potential for great harm, but it is still too soon to see how greatly Lake Erie and its fish life will be affected.

Absolute stability is not ever likely to come to the Great Lakes. But there can be no doubt that cleaner water has already come. This, combined with the many exciting new game fish that have been introduced, has brought on a spectacular renewal of interest in fishing in all the Great Lakes. It could be said that Erie was the last in the chain to enjoy this renaissance. But now it is offering up some of the best sport fishing in North America.

No one is laughing at Lake Erie any more.